lonely planet

Diving & Snorkeling

Florida Keys

William Harrigan

LONELY PLANET PUBLICATIONS
Melbourne • Oakland • London • Paris

Diving & Snorkeling Florida Keys
- A Lonely Planet Pisces Book

3rd Edition – August 2001
2nd Edition – 1993 Gulf Publishing Company
1st Edition – 1984 Pisces Books Inc.

Published by
Lonely Planet Publications
90 Maribyrnong St., Footscray, Victoria 3011, Australia

Other offices
150 Linden Street, Oakland, California 94607, USA
10a Spring Place, London NW5 3BH, UK
1 rue du Dahomey, 75011 Paris, France

Photographs
by William Harrigan (unless otherwise noted)

Front cover photograph
In the wheelhouse of the *Duane*, Upper Keys

Back cover photographs
Christ of the Deep, Key Largo Dry Rocks, Upper Keys
Deepwater sea fan and sponges, Looe Key (Deep),
    Lower Keys
Reef and Long Key Viaduct, Overseas Highway,
    Middle Keys

Most of the images in this guide are available for
    licensing from **Lonely Planet Images**
email: lpi@lonelyplanet.com.au

ISBN 0 86442 774 3

text & maps © Lonely Planet 2001
photographs © photographers as indicated 2001
dive site maps are Transverse Mercator projection

LONELY PLANET and the Lonely Planet logo are
trademarks of Lonely Planet Publications Pty Ltd.

Printed by H&Y Printing Ltd., Hong Kong

Contents

Introduction   **9**

Overview   **11**

Geography 11
Geology 11
Ecology 12
History 14

Practicalities   **18**

Climate 18
Language 18
Getting There 19
Gateway City – Miami 19
Getting Around 21
Time 22
Money 22
Electricity 22
Weights & Measures 22
What to Bring 23
Underwater Photography 23
Business Hours 24
Accommodations 25
Dining & Food 25
Shopping 26

Activities & Attractions   **27**

Glass-Bottom Boats 27
Kayaking & Canoeing 27
Parasailing 28
Dolphin Encounters 28
Fishing 29
Sailing 30
Florida State Parks & Recreation Areas 30
Key West Aquarium 30

Maritime Museums 30
Sunset Celebration 31

Diving Health & Safety 32

Pre-Trip Preparation 32
DAN 34
Medical & Recompression Facilities 35

Diving in the Florida Keys 36

Dive Training & Certification 37
Snorkeling 38
Live-Aboards 39
Pisces Rating System for Dives & Divers 40

Biscayne National Park Dive Sites 42

1 Long Reef. 43
2 Virginia Reef 44
3 The Wall 45

Upper Keys Dive Sites 46

Key Largo 47

4 Turtle Rocks 50
5 Carysfort Reef. 51
6 South Carysfort Reef 52
7 Civil War Wreck 53
8 City of Washington 54
9 The Elbow. 55
10 Horseshoe Reef 56
11 North North Dry Rocks. 57
12 North Dry Rocks. 58
13 Key Largo Dry Rocks 59
14 Grecian Rocks (Fore Reef). 60
15 Grecian Rocks (Back Reef). 61
16 Spiegel Grove. 62
17 Benwood 64
18 French Reef 65
19 White Bank (North & South). 66

20 Three Sisters. 66

21 Sand Island 67

22 Molasses Reef (North End) 68

23 Molasses Reef (Deep). 70

24 Molasses Reef (South End) 71

25 *Bibb* 72

26 *Duane* 73

27 Pickles 74

Plantation & Upper Matecumbe Keys   **75**

28 Conch Wall 77

29 Conch Reef 78

30 Hen & Chickens 80

31 Davis Reef 81

32 Crocker Reef 82

33 *Eagle* 82

34 Alligator Reef. 84

Middle Keys Dive Sites   **85**

35 Coffins Patch 87

36 *Thunderbolt*. 88

37 The Gap. 89

38 Samatha's Reef. 90

39 Herman's Hole 91

40 Flagler's Barge 92

41 Delta Shoal 93

42 Sombrero Reef 94

Lower Keys & Key West Dive Sites   **95**

43 Newfound Harbor 98

44 Looe Key (East End) 98

45 Looe Key (West End) 99

46 Looe Key (Deep) 100

47 *Adolphus Busch Sr.*. 102

48 Western Sambo 103

49 Joe's Tug 105

50 Toppino's Buoy. 106

51 9-Foot Stake 107

52 *Cayman Salvage Master* 108

53 Eastern Dry Rocks. 109

54 Rock Key 110

55 Sand Key Reef 111

56 Western Dry Rocks. 112

57 Marquesas Keys 113

Dry Tortugas Dive Sites   114

58 Sherwood Forest 116

59 Texas Rock. 117

60 Fort Jefferson Moat Wall. 118

61 Windjammer 119

Marine Life   120

Hazardous Marine Life 123

Diving Conservation & Awareness   126

Marine Reserves & Regulations 126

Responsible Diving 129

Listings   132

Telephone Calls 132

Diving Services. 132

Live-Aboards 138

State Parks. 138

Chambers of Commerce 139

Index   141

Author

Bill Harrigan

A former manager of the Key Largo National Marine Sanctuary, Bill Harrigan made his first dive in the Florida Keys in 1971. He later earned a master's degree in marine park management and directed the U.S. National Marine Sanctuary Program in Washington, D.C. In 1993 Bill became a professional writer and photographer and founded Ocean Life Enterprises (www.oceanlifeenterprises.com), an international marine park management consultancy. He has written and taken photos for more than 150 articles, many about the Florida Keys, for popular dive magazines.

From the Author

Thank you to the many friends in the Florida Keys who assisted me in preparing this guide. I am especially indebted to my wife, Kathleen, and to Steve Frink, Mike and Heidi Waters, Liz Johnson, Joe Clark, Doc Schweinler, Craig Nappier, Spencer and Annette Slate, Rob Haff, Jeff Cleary, Scott Rodman, Paul Caputo, Rob Bleser, Amy Slate, Steve Baumgardner, Cheva Heck, Ben Richards, John and Judy Halas, Brenda Altmeier, Mary Tagliareni, Dave Savage, Bill and Heidi Ferrell, Joe Glenn, Remy Cabrera, David Taylor, DeeVon Quirolo, Chris Bors, Jackie Bors, Laura Woods, Brendan Kerr, Patrick Kerr, Marie Stallings and Dave Harrigan.

Photography Notes

Underwater, Bill Harrigan uses a variety of cameras, including three Nikonos Vs, a Nikonos RS and a Nikon F4 in an Aquatica housing. For macro and close-up photography he prefers 50mm, 60mm and 105mm macro lenses with Ikelite strobes, while using 13mm, 15mm, 16mm and 18mm lenses with both Nikon and Ikelite strobes for wide-angle photography. Topside, Bill works with the Nikon F100 and a variety of lenses. He uses Kodak Ektachrome 100S and Fuji Velvia color slide film.

Contributing Photographers

Bill Harrigan took most of the photographs in this book. Thanks also to the U.S. Naval Institute and Jules' Undersea Lodge.

From the Publisher

This third edition was published in Lonely Planet's U.S. office under the guidance of Roslyn Bullas, the Pisces Books publishing manager. David Lauterborn edited the text and photos with buddy checks from Sarah Hubbard and Erin Corrigan. Emily Douglas designed the cover and book. Navigating the nautical charts was cartographer Sara Nelson with assistance from Rachel Driver, Brad Lodge and Gina Gillich. U.S. cartography manager Alex Guilbert supervised map production. Justin Marler illustrated the Conch Republic flag and amended the marine sanctuaries illustration. Lindsay Brown reviewed the Marine Life section for scientific accuracy. Portions of the text were adapted from Lonely Planet's *Florida*.

Pisces Pre-Dive Safety Guidelines

Before embarking on a scuba diving, skin diving or snorkeling trip, carefully consider the following to help ensure a safe and enjoyable experience:

- Possess a current diving certification card from a recognized scuba diving instructional agency (if scuba diving)
- Be sure you are healthy and feel comfortable diving
- Obtain reliable information about physical and environmental conditions at the dive site (e.g., from a reputable local dive operation)
- Be aware of local laws, regulations and etiquette about marine life and environment
- Dive at sites within your experience level; if possible, engage the services of a competent, professionally trained dive instructor or divemaster

Underwater conditions vary significantly from one region, or even site, to another. Seasonal changes can significantly alter site and dive conditions. These differences influence the way divers dress for a dive and what diving techniques they use.

There are special requirements for diving in any area, regardless of location. Before your dive, ask about environmental characteristics that can affect your diving and how trained local divers deal with these considerations.

Warning & Request

Things change—dive site conditions, regulations, topside information. Nothing stays the same for long. Your feedback on this book will be used to help update and improve the next edition. Excerpts from your correspondence may appear in *Planet Talk*, our quarterly newsletter, or *Comet*, our monthly email newsletter. Please let us know if you do not want your letter published or your name acknowledged.

Correspondence can be addressed to:
Lonely Planet Publications
Pisces Books
150 Linden Street
Oakland, CA 94607
email: pisces@lonelyplanet.com

Introduction

The range of diving and snorkeling opportunities in the Florida Keys is exceptional. There's something here for everyone—from novice snorkelers to seasoned divers with hundreds of hours under their weight belts. Snorkelers will enjoy the many shallow reef crests, where you simply float on the surface surrounded by colorful reef fish and view the lovely corals a few feet below. Divers of all skill levels explore the same reefs in depths from 15 to 35 feet (5 to 11m), while experienced divers tour the coral-covered slopes between 35 and 70 feet (11 and 21m). Advanced divers will appreciate the extraordinary marine life in the region and can hone their skills on many deeper wrecks and reefs.

Don't expect to find miles of wide sandy beach here, however. There are a few nice beaches in Key West and the Dry Tortugas, and several resorts have even imported their own small beaches. But the expansive beaches of the Florida mainland stop after Key Biscayne. That's OK, though, because no one from the Keys would trade their coral reefs for a beach.

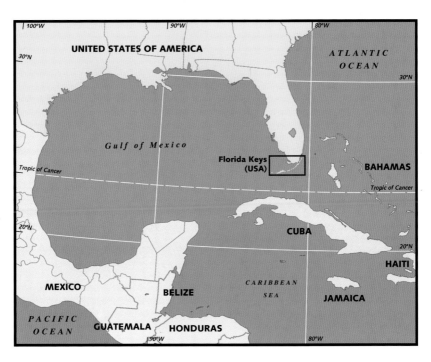

You can reach nearly everywhere but the reefs themselves by car. It's a scenic trip, too, especially after you cover the 30 or so miles (about 50km) from Miami International Airport to the end of Florida's Turnpike at Florida City. You "officially" start your drive to the Florida Keys at this point. The view out either side of the car is great from here all the way to Key West, though traffic is frequently slow, and passing is often restricted. Your best bet is to relax, allow plenty of time to get to your destination, and enjoy the ride.

This book covers sites from Biscayne Bay to Fort Jefferson, including **Biscayne National Park**, the **Upper Keys**, the **Middle Keys**, the **Lower Keys & Key West** and the remote **Dry Tortugas**. You'll find specific information on 61 of the best sites in the Florida Keys, including location, depth, access and recommended diving expertise. You'll also learn about each site's underwater terrain and the marine life you may encounter. The Marine Life section even offers a preview of the Keys' most common vertebrates and invertebrates. While the book is not intended as a stand-alone travel guide, the Overview and Practicalities sections provide useful information about the islands, and the Activities & Attractions section offers tips on unique topside pursuits along the Overseas Highway.

Perhaps nowhere else in the world does watching the sunset take on such ritual significance.

Overview

High on many divers' lifetime list of places to go, the Florida Keys are a complex ecosystem of islands, mangroves, hardwood hammocks, pinelands, seagrass beds, coral reefs, bays and open ocean. The archipelago dangles from the Florida mainland like an emerald necklace, connected by a slender, 107-mile (172km) ribbon of highway. The three largest towns, Key Largo, Marathon and Key West, are spaced about equally along the Overseas Highway, with smaller developments such as Tavernier, Layton, Big Pine Key and Summerland Key interspersed between them.

Each year more than 4 million tourists outnumber the 80,000 or so permanent residents of the Keys. Summer is considered the off-season, but visitation levels are nearly the same year-round these days. Even so, the pace is still easy and the lifestyle informal. For every silk tie there are a thousand cotton T-shirts; for every pair of high heels, a thousand pairs of sandals.

Most of the natural resources that draw visitors to the Keys are not on the developed islands, but in the surrounding waters and nature refuges of the uninhabited islands. Out there, beneath the surface of the clear, warm water, is the treasure so many of us come to see.

Geography

The Keys arc away from the southeastern tip of Florida in a sweeping curve, heading south at first, then gradually turning west. The Upper Keys are flanked on the west by Florida Bay, a shallow body of water dotted with hundreds of small, uninhabited mangrove islands. To the east is the Atlantic Ocean, with the closest islands of The Bahamas about 60 miles (95km) distant. Key West is the southernmost point in the continental U.S. Next stop is Cuba, about 90 miles (145km) across the Straits of Florida. North of Key West are the eastern shores of the Gulf of Mexico.

Geology

Basking in the warm Florida sun, you'll find it difficult to imagine that glacial activity shaped these islands. Although the process has been occurring over millions of years, the geologic history of the Keys began about 125,000 years ago, when melting ice raised sea levels by 20ft (6m) or more. The Upper and Lower Keys began to form about that time, but by two different methods. Reefs flourished in the waters of the Upper and Middle Keys, their coral polyps depositing calcium carbonate that rose atop a limestone foundation. In the Lower Keys, large deposits of a crystalline precipitate called oolite settled, creating a somewhat different foundation.

As glaciers again froze, sea levels dropped, leaving the oolite and coral reefs high and dry long enough to form the islands we walk on today. About 75,000 years ago the sea rose once more, and another chain of reefs grew along the shelf edge, bathed by the warm Gulf Stream waters. These reefs died when the sea fell yet again about 30,000 years ago, though their fossilized structures would provide the foundation of our present-day reefs.

About 10,000 years ago the sea returned, filling a trench that would become Hawk Channel. It also filled in Florida Bay and gave birth to the Everglades. Five or six thousand years ago, the water reached its present level, and the coral reefs we know began to grow again along the shelf. Topsoil accumulated on the islands, followed by vegetation and finally human life.

Nature's Watercolors

The palette of colors in these waters ranges from a stunning deep blue to a chalky green, depending on the location and weather conditions. The outer reefs are closer to the Gulf Stream and normally benefit from its warm, clear water. The inshore reefs and Florida Bay are usually bathed in the more nutrient-rich and slightly cooler green water associated with coastal circulation. Often the two sources will mix along the reef line, coloring the water blue-green. This mixing may be quite distinct, so that one reef will boast blue water while another nearby is tinged blue-green. During rough weather, the water can take on a milky cast. Fortunately, this condition is fleeting, and the water quickly clears.

Ecology

Divers find two basic reef structures in the Florida Keys: patch reefs and bank reefs. There are literally thousands of patch reefs, most of them small and unnamed. Relatively close to shore, these reefs are generally oval, with an extremely shallow, flat reeftop and sloping sides. The surrounding sand flats can be anywhere from 5 to 30 feet (2 to 9m) deep. Nearshore circulation tinges the water blue-green. Bank reefs skirt the edge of the broad shallow slope adjacent to deep water 4 to 6 miles (6 to 10km) offshore. These are large, more complex structures that extend from the surface to 80 or 90ft (24 or 27m). Blue to blue-green offshore water is common.

Often mistaken for rocks and plants, corals are actually colonial animals. Each colony contains thousands of tiny individuals called polyps, which live on the surface of a structure composed of their predecessors' excretions. This structure may be hard and shaped like branches or mounds, or soft and shaped like fans or whips.

Most coral colonies grow slowly, but their longevity can be phenomenal. Star corals, for instance, expand about a half inch (1cm) in diameter per year. The largest star corals in the Keys are about 10 to 13ft (3 to 4m) in diameter, which puts their age in excess of 300 years. Branching corals, like elkhorn and staghorn, grow the fastest. Under favorable conditions an elkhorn branch may grow up to 4 inches (10cm) per year.

Algae is essential to coral reefs in two ways. First, it provides much of the energy that keeps corals alive. Living symbiotically within the tissues of coral polyps, algae called zooxanthellae rely on photosynthesis to produce energy, which in turn sustains the coral—part of the reason corals flourish in clear, shallow water. Second, algae provides food for the many herbivores that live on the reef. However, algae can also be an impediment to reef health, as it grows faster than coral and often outcompetes it for space.

There is as much sponge life as coral on a reef, sometimes even more. In addition to being a principal food source for many reef inhabitants, sponges filter the water, improving visibility. Several sponges grow in distinctive shapes, such as tube, barrel and finger sponges. Others have no particular shape, but encrust solid structures like coral colonies, wrecks and other objects.

Like their terrestrial counterparts, seagrasses have a sophisticated root system. Two species grow in abundance in the Keys: flat-bladed turtle grass and round-bladed eel grass. Seagrass is a vital component of the coral reef ecosystem, providing food

Sponges serve as both water filters and food source.

for herbivores, nursery grounds for juvenile reef fish and habitat for thousands of invertebrate species, as well as binding sediments and oxygenating the water. A quick tour of seagrass beds will turn up such animals as tritons and queen and helmet conchs.

Mangrove forests are also stabilizers. They have adapted to grow in salt water, their long roots anchoring the sediment along the shoreline. In fact, the shoreline itself is stabilized by mangroves, even in the face of hurricanes. Three species of mangrove are found in the Keys: red, white and black. The most common species, red mangroves are sometimes called the "walking trees" for their long, open root system and propensity for shallow water.

Mangroves offer habitat to marine life and birds.

History

The Keys' earliest residents were Indians referred to variously by European explorers as Matecumbes, Biscaynos, Tequestas and Calusas. They were nomadic tribes who traversed the coast in wooden dugouts, or pirogues, living on fish, turtles, manatees and shellfish. Pottery and middens consisting of discarded fish bones and conch shells date back prior to 1000 BC.

The Spaniards discovered the Florida Keys in 1513, when Ponce de León sailed through the islands in his search for the mythical Fountain of Youth. He called the islands *Los Martires* (The Martyrs), because their twisted shapes reminded him of martyred Christians. With little fresh water for its ships and no treasure to plunder, the Keys were of little interest to Spain and remained largely forgotten during the next two and a half centuries.

During the 1700s, many Bahamians crossed the Straits of Florida to cut wood and catch turtles in the Keys. The families that stayed survived largely by eating queen conch, the large gastropod that could be found in abundance. The people themselves came to be called Conchs (pronounced Konks), a sobriquet longtime Keys residents still proudly apply to themselves.

In 1821, John Simonton bought Key West from Juan Pablo Salas of Spain for $2,000—not as good a deal as Manhattan or Alaska perhaps, but still one of the all-time best real estate bargains. With a good deepwater port, Key West quickly became the first viable settlement in the Keys.

As the volume of goods being shipped between the Mississippi and the East Coast increased in the early 1800s, the waters of the Florida Keys became a shipping highway. Many ships came to grief on the shallow reefs, some as a result of a lucrative new industry called "wrecking." Based out of Key West, wreckers were a wild group of men who sailed out to strip grounded ships of their cargo. They would often hasten the trade by stringing up lanterns on shore, luring ships onto the reefs. Between 1830 and 1840 alone, more than 300 ships ran aground off the Florida Keys.

The wrecking trade became less profitable in the 1850s, when the reefs were permanently marked by a string of lighthouses. Utilizing a new "screw-pile" design that allowed construction of an open-framed structure directly on the reef, these lighthouses continue to operate today on Sand Key, American Shoal, Sombrero Reef, Alligator Reef, Carysfort Reef and Fowey Rocks.

In the latter half of the 19th century other industries such as sponging and turtle hunting flourished in the Keys. Even farming was briefly successful, as homesteaders harvested melons, coconuts and pineapples. Shallow-draft boats ferried the produce to Key West, where it was loaded onto schooners bound for northern ports.

The face of the region changed forever when Henry Flagler, president of the Florida East Coast Railway, decided to extend his railroad from Miami to Key West in 1905. The Overseas Railroad took seven years and $27 million to construct, a huge expense that garnered the project the nickname "Flagler's Folly." Work crews were plagued by heat, lack of fresh water and mosquitoes as they built the bridges and embankments needed to connect the islands. The railroad was finally completed, but operated for 23 years without ever turning a profit.

Disaster struck on September 2, 1935, when a massive hurricane battered the Keys. The storm's 18ft (5m) tidal wave and 200mph (320km/h) winds killed 800 people and wiped out both the railroad and any thoughts of rebuilding it. The railroad went into receivership, and the government bought the right-of-way and bridges for just $640,000.

For the next three years ferries transported cars from island to island as the railroad bridges were widened for use by automobiles. In March 1938 the Overseas Highway was officially opened, making the Florida Keys the most accessible archipelago in the world.

Three other developments secured a future for the Keys. The first was the establishment of military airfields and ship bases in Key West and Marathon during WWII. The second was the completion of a 130-mile (210km) pipeline from Florida City to Key West to bring fresh water to the Keys. Without airfields, ports and fresh water, life here would be a difficult proposition indeed. The third advancement was not change, but protection. Initiated in the early '60s, a network of marine parks, sanctuaries and refuges has blossomed to protect all of the Keys' natural resources.

Florida Keys

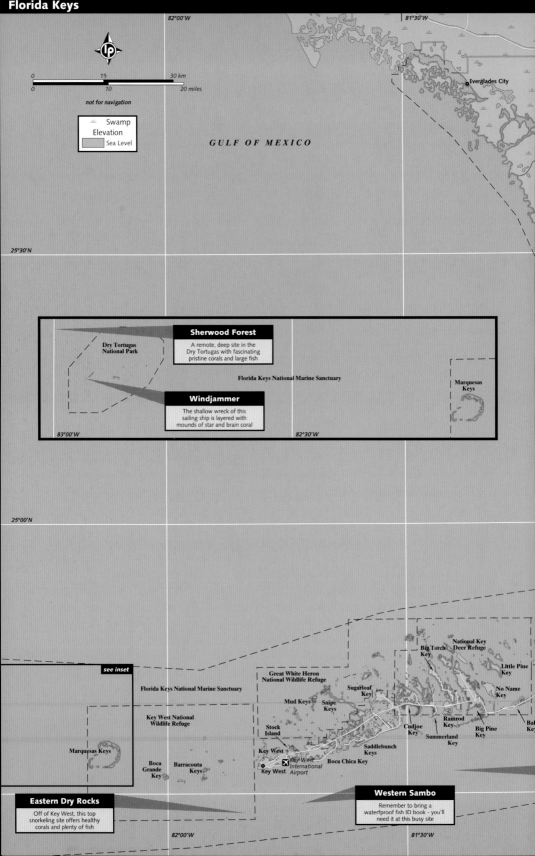

not for navigation

Swamp
Elevation
Sea Level

GULF OF MEXICO

82°00'W

81°30'W

● Everglades City

25°30'N

Sherwood Forest
A remote, deep site in the Dry Tortugas with fascinating pristine corals and large fish

Dry Tortugas
National Park

Florida Keys National Marine Sanctuary

Marquesas
Keys

Windjammer
The shallow wreck of this sailing ship is layered with mounds of star and brain coral

83°00'W

82°30'W

25°00'N

see inset

Florida Keys National Marine Sanctuary

Key West National
Wildlife Refuge

Marquesas Keys

Boca
Grande
Key

Barracouta
Keys

Great White Heron
National Wildlife Refuge

Mud Keys

Snipe
Keys

Sugarloaf
Key

Big Torch
Key

National Key
Deer Refuge

Little Pine
Key

No Name
Key

Stock
Island

Key West

Key West
International
Airport

Boca Chica Key

Saddlebunch
Keys

Cudjoe
Key

Ramrod
Key

Summerland
Key

Big Pine
Key

Bah
Key

Eastern Dry Rocks
Off of Key West, this top snorkeling site offers healthy corals and plenty of fish

Western Sambo
Remember to bring a waterproof fish ID book - you'll need it at this busy site

82°00'W

81°30'W

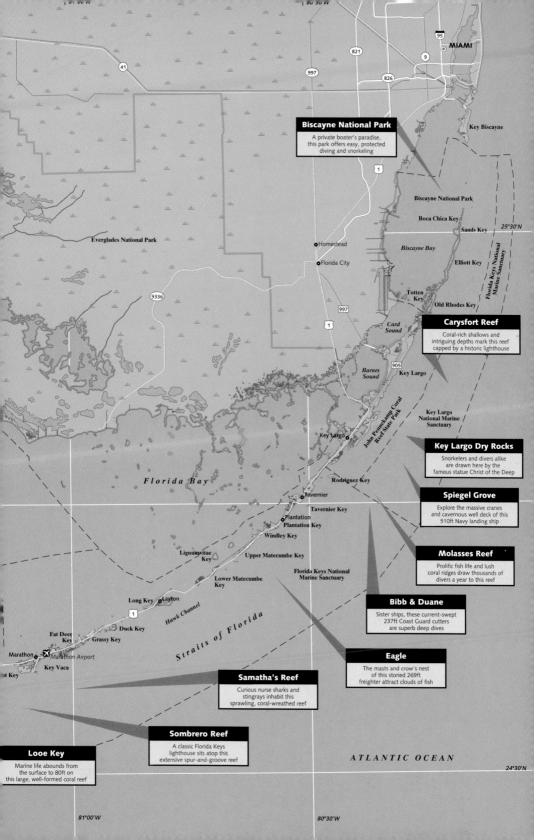

Biscayne National Park

A private boater's paradise, this park offers easy, protected diving and snorkeling

Carysfort Reef

Coral-rich shallows and intriguing depths mark this reef capped by a historic lighthouse

Key Largo Dry Rocks

Snorkelers and divers alike are drawn here by the famous statue Christ of the Deep

Spiegel Grove

Explore the massive cranes and cavernous well deck of this 510ft Navy landing ship

Molasses Reef

Prolific fish life and lush coral ridges draw thousands of divers a year to this reef

Bibb & Duane

Sister ships, these current-swept 237ft Coast Guard cutters are superb deep dives

Eagle

The masts and crow's nest of this storied 269ft freighter attract clouds of fish

Samatha's Reef

Curious nurse sharks and stingrays inhabit this sprawling, coral-wreathed reef

Sombrero Reef

A classic Florida Keys lighthouse sits atop this extensive spur-and-groove reef

Looe Key

Marine life abounds from the surface to 80ft on this large, well-formed coral reef

MIAMI

Key Biscayne

Biscayne National Park

Boca Chica Key

Sands Key

25°30'N

Elliott Key

Totten Key

Old Rhodes Key

Florida Keys National Marine Sanctuary

Everglades National Park

Homestead

Florida City

Biscayne Bay

Card Sound

Barnes Sound

Key Largo

Key Largo

Key Largo National Marine Sanctuary

John Pennekamp Coral Reef State Park

Florida Bay

Rodriguez Key

Tavernier

Tavernier Key

Plantation

Plantation Key

Windley Key

Lignumvitae Key

Upper Matecumbe Key

Lower Matecumbe Key

Florida Keys National Marine Sanctuary

Long Key

Layton

Duck Key

Hawk Channel

Fat Deer Key

Grassy Key

Straits of Florida

Marathon

Marathon Airport

Key Vaca

ot Key

ATLANTIC OCEAN

24°30'N

81°00'W

80°30'W

Practicalities

Climate

The Florida Keys boast a tropical climate, even though the islands lie about 75 miles (120km) north of the Tropic of Cancer, the usual dividing line between the tropics and the rest of the Northern Hemisphere. The secret is the Gulf Stream, that vast current of warm ocean water that blesses the Keys with both clear water and good weather. Visitors often ask residents, "Don't you miss the seasons?" However, the climate in the Keys does change as the year progresses, even though winter in South Florida may seem like summer in more northern latitudes.

Average high temperatures in the winter are about 75°F (24°C), dropping to around 65°F (18°C) at night. Cold spells lasting three or four days may set in occasionally, dropping temperatures into the 50s Fahrenheit (10 to 15°C). Daytime highs in the summer average about 90°F (32°C). Relative humidity is high throughout the year, averaging about 75%. Water temperatures range from 73 to 76°F (23 to 24°C) in the winter, rising to between 83 and 86°F (28 and 30°C) in the summer.

The southeast trade winds are a permanent feature of Florida Keys weather, but they vary in strength throughout the year. They are strongest in the winter, often blowing at 10 to 20 knots (12 to 24mph; 19 to 38km/h). In summer the trade winds slack off, often dropping to a flat calm.

The wet season lasts from May to October, accounting for about three-quarters of the total annual rainfall. Rain during this period usually falls in brief but intense early-morning or late-afternoon showers. The exception to this pattern is rain associated with tropical storms, which can bring longer periods of inclement weather. The dry season lasts from November to April.

Hurricane season officially begins June 1 and runs through the end of November, though most storms occur in September and October. Unless a hurricane or tropical storm is actually threatening the Keys, however, the weather is generally very good for diving during this period. Hurricane watches or warnings should be taken seriously, as there is little protection from high winds or storm surge if one should strike.

Language

English is the primary language of the Florida Keys, though you may also frequently see and hear Spanish. Road signs are in English, but informational signs may include a Spanish translation. Recognizing that many visitors are from overseas, some dive shops have instructors on staff who speak other languages, including German, French and Japanese.

Getting There

Most visitors to the Florida Keys travel via Miami or Fort Lauderdale by rental car or tour bus. Driving time from Miami International Airport to Key Largo is about an hour and a half. Marathon is about two and a half hours from Miami, while Key West is three and a half to four hours from Miami.

To reach the Keys from Miami, get on Florida's Turnpike Extension headed south. At Florida City the turnpike ends, funneling you onto U.S. 1 South. Immediately after Florida City you have a choice: take Card Sound Road or continue south on U.S. 1. The Card Sound route is slightly longer and has a toll bridge, but there's also less traffic. U.S. 1 is shorter, but includes the dreaded "18-mile stretch," which can back up with slow traffic. Either way you'll end up on Key Largo.

There are also direct flights to Key West International Airport, with connections from Orlando, Fort Myers, Naples, Fort Lauderdale or Miami. Limited connections are also available to Marathon. Rental cars are available in Key Largo, Marathon and Key West.

Gateway City – Miami

With a population of 1.9 million and one of the world's busiest airports, Miami is a major city and popular tourist destination. The Miami area comprises many distinctive cultural zones, such as South Beach (SoBe), Coconut Grove, Little Havana, Key Biscayne and Coral Gables, each offering its own attractions, art and flavor.

Miami is also a great city for sports fans. Football teams include the Miami Dolphins and University of Miami Hurricanes; in major-league baseball it's the Marlins; and in hockey, the Panthers. The annual Lipton Championship features pro tennis at Crandon Park on Key Biscayne. Horse racing fans have two venues: Hialeah Racetrack and Calder Race Course. Jai alai and auto racing round out the area's professional sports. Naturally, the long sandy beaches and blue Atlantic Ocean are also favorites with visitors.

Seven major malls head the nearly endless shopping

Miami Beach boasts the sand, sea, hotels and clubs.

opportunities in Miami. Smaller shops in South Beach and Coconut Grove offer original works of art and jewelry. Accommodations, restaurants and nightlife abound, particularly in SoBe.

Getting Around

Rental cars are by far the most popular mode of transportation among visitors to the Keys. The Overseas Highway is an easy drive, and except in Key West, free parking is readily available. A car can be a necessity for divers, since many dive shops and boats are not based at the hotels.

Taxis operate throughout the Keys, providing local service as well as transportation to and from Miami. Arrangements should be made in advance for transportation to and from the Miami and Fort Lauderdale airports. Check the yellow pages for taxi and limousine listings.

A bike path runs intermittently alongside the Overseas Highway. It is continuous through Key Largo, but terminates just north of Tavernier, reappearing at intervals between Tavernier and Key West. Use caution on the bike path, as motorists are often oblivious to bicycles and fail to yield the right of way. Bike helmets are not required by Florida law, but wearing one is highly recommended. Key West is reasonably bike friendly, particularly if you stay on designated bike paths. Rental bikes are available in Key Largo, Marathon and Key West, with models ranging from single-speed beach cruisers to sophisticated mountain bikes.

Rental mopeds are also a popular mode of transportation in Key West, where parking can be at a premium. Ride cautiously—other motorists may not see you.

Follow the Trail of MMs

The Overseas Highway (U.S. 1) is the only road from Key Largo to Key West. Directions to places along the highway are given by specifying the mile marker (MM) and often which side of the road, as in MM 49.2 oceanside or MM 99 bayside. In addition to these simple directions, you may hear people refer to the Upper, Middle and Lower Keys. These are general divisions, unofficial but useful when talking about what goes on where. In this book the Upper Keys include the islands from Key Largo to Long Key (MM 107 to MM 66), the Middle Keys from the Long Key Viaduct to Vaca Key (MM 65 to MM 47), and the Lower Keys from the Seven Mile Bridge to Key West (MM 46 to MM 0)—though locals often refer to Key West (MM 12 to MM 0) as a separate entity.

Rental boats are available throughout the Keys, but are recommended for experienced boaters only. Navigation can be tricky, and running aground will be expensive. If you want to rent a boat, but don't feel confident about navigating in the Keys, go out once or twice with a dive operator first to get a feel for the area. When you do take a boat out, be sure you have a large-scale chart and know how to read it.

Time

The Florida Keys are on Eastern Standard Time and, like most of the U.S., observe daylight saving time. When it's noon in the Florida Keys, it's 9am in San Francisco, 5pm in London and 4am the following day in Sydney.

Money

U.S. dollars are the only accepted currency. Major credit cards are accepted nearly everywhere, including rental-car agencies, hotels, restaurants, gas stations and many supermarkets. Traveler's checks are also widely accepted. Automatic teller machines (ATMs) are available in the major towns.

The state sales tax is 6% on all purchases. In Miami the value-added tax is 6.5%, with an additional 5% tax on hotel accommodations (or 11.5% total tax on hotels).

Tipping is customary for good service. Be aware that a 15% tip may already be included in your restaurant bill. Restaurant waitstaff and taxi drivers should receive 10 to 20% of the tab. Bellhops should be given about $1 per bag, while hotel maids should be tipped at least $1.50 a day.

Electricity

Electricity throughout the U.S. is 110-115 volts, 60 Hz AC. Most outlets accept ungrounded plugs with two parallel blades (one slightly larger than the other) or grounded plugs with two parallel blades and a rounded shaft. Though several stores sell transformers and adapters, it's best to bring your own for dive light and strobe batteries.

Weights & Measures

The imperial system of weights and measures is used throughout the U.S., although metric equivalents are sometimes supplied. Distances are in feet, yards and miles. Weights are in ounces, pounds and tons. Please refer to the conversion chart on the inside back cover for metric equivalents.

In dive shops and aboard dive boats, distances are given in nautical miles, weights are given in pounds, air pressure is measured in pounds per square inch (PSI) and depths are given in feet. Divers accustomed to the metric system should expect to perform their own conversions.

In this book both imperial and metric measurements are given, except for specific references in dive site descriptions, which are given in imperial units only.

What to Bring
General

The dress code in the Florida Keys is informal. Pack mostly shorts, short-sleeved shirts and T-shirts. Sneakers or sandals are fine, but many dive shops discourage flip-flops on their boats or docks, as they can slip off one's foot. Sport sandals that fasten securely at heel and toe are a better choice. A lightweight jacket, sweater or long pants may be needed in winter months, especially in the evening, and a sweatshirt or warm-up suit is nice to have for the boat ride back from a dive.

Wide-brimmed hats offer excellent protection from the sun. Sunglasses with UV protection are a good idea on the water, as are polarizing sunglasses, which reduce reflected glare. Also bring plenty of waterproof sunblock and insect repellent.

Dive-Related

Pack your C-card first. Getting faxed verification from your certifying agency is often possible, but waiting for a response may delay your dive plans. Also bring your logbook. Aside from being able to keep your entries up to date, you may need to show evidence of recent diving experience for the more advanced or deep dives.

Bring several bathing suits, so you'll always have a dry one to start the day. Stretchy lycra suits fit better than baggy trunks beneath wetsuits.

Most dive shops carry a full range of rental wetsuits, although bringing your own is always a good idea. A bathing suit or lycra dive skin is sufficient during summer months, when water temperatures reach 86°F (30°C). Shorty wetsuits are popular year-round, though a 3mm full suit is a better option in the spring and fall or if you get cold easily. In the winter, water temperatures dip as low as 73°F (23°C), and a 5mm full suit is needed to keep warm.

Hands Off

Wearing gloves is discouraged in the Florida Keys, as divers with gloves tend to have more contact with the coral. Gloves aren't needed for warmth, so rather than wear them for protection from coral cuts, it's better to keep your hands off the live coral and learn what you can safely touch. Wearing gloves is often prudent on wrecks, though, which may have sharp edges and surfaces coated with fire coral and stinging hydroids.

Underwater Photography

Three factors make the Keys one of the best locations in the world for underwater photography: reasonably clear water, countless underwater subjects and excellent photo services. The visibility is nearly always workable for wide-angle photography and is often very good. Typical reef topography lends itself to wide-angle setups, with interesting foregrounds and backgrounds. Thousands of approachable fish present endless opportunities for normal lens photography. Macro, of course, is always a good choice, no matter what the weather. Night dives in the Keys are great for normal shots, portraits or macrophotography.

Photo services available include one-hour processing for print film and next-day processing for slides. Film and batteries are widely available, and several shops can make basic repairs to underwater cameras, strobes or housings. Photo equipment rentals range from basic cameras like the Sea & Sea MX-5 to Nikonos V rigs with strobe and wide-angle lens.

Remember to rinse your camera after every dive.

Underwater photography equipment, including several brands of housings, is available at competitive prices. Several photo businesses and dive shops offer classes in underwater photography.

Support services, rentals and instruction are also available for underwater videography. Housed compact digital cameras are rented by the day, and several shops offer custom underwater videos of your dive.

Business Hours

Extended operating hours are normal for most businesses in the Keys, including weekends. Round-the-clock service is available at many gas stations, hotels and convenience stores. Supermarkets generally open at 7am and close at 9 or 10pm. Some restaurants are open only for breakfast and lunch, with service from 6am to 2pm. Fast-food restaurants begin breakfast service at 6:30am and switch to their lunch menu at 10:30 on weekdays and 11:30 on weekends. Most of the national franchises stay open until 10pm; some operate drive-through windows until 1am.

Dive shops usually open their doors at 8am. The morning trip leaves the dock at 8:30 or 9, and the shops remain open till the last boat returns, sometime between 5 and 7pm.

Accommodations

A full range of accommodations, from basic to indulgent luxury, are available in the Keys. At the budget end of the scale, campgrounds provide tent and RV sites for modest fees. You'll find single rooms, studios, suites, condos, time-shares and houses in nearly every price range. Prices vary according to the time of year, with high season running from December 30 to March 30.

Accommodations are clustered around the population centers, particularly Key Largo, Islamorada, Marathon, Big Pine Key and Key West. However, some motels, time-shares and smaller inns are available outside of these centers.

Advance reservations are highly recommended, especially during the winter months and in Key West. Hotels often fill early, but travel agents can usually find you alternative accommodations if your first choice is booked.

Seabed & Breakfast

Most of us are fascinated by the notion of staying underwater for long periods—even living underwater. At Jules' Undersea Lodge you can stay underwater from check-in at 1pm until checkout at 11am, or even stay for several days. Open since 1986, the lodge is a luxury undersea habitat set in a natural mangrove lagoon 30ft (9m) deep. Originally constructed as an undersea research laboratory in the 1970s, the habitat was used for research projects on the continental shelf off Puerto Rico. Refurbished with modern guest amenities, the lodge gives visitors to the Florida Keys a unique opportunity to experience an extended stay beneath the surface. Unlimited diving is included, using 120ft (37m) hookah rigs. Noncertified divers can take a three-hour Discover Diving class to qualify for entry. Dinner and breakfast are included in all three of the available lodging packages.

Jules' Undersea Lodge
MM 103.2
51 Shoreland Drive
Key Largo
☎ 305-451-2353
fax: 305-451-4789
www.jul.com
info@jul.com

Dining & Food

You'll find restaurants covering a range of dining experiences in the Keys. Naturally, waterfront dining is readily available, and many restaurants offer truly fresh seafood. Tropical and Cuban influences are also reflected in the cuisine. The popular fast-food chains have outlets in Key Largo, Tavernier, Marathon and

Key West if you feel the need for speed, and there are many small, quaint places unique to the Keys.

Look for large supermarkets, like Publix and Winn Dixie, in Key Largo, Tavernier, Marathon, Big Pine Key and Key West. All of these stores have extended hours. Smaller convenience stores, such as Circle K and Tom Thumb, are located every few miles along the highway. Of course, the selection of goods is much smaller than at supermarkets, and the prices are generally higher, but many convenience stores are open 24 hours, seven days a week.

Don't leave without sampling at least one of the conch dishes for which the Keys are famous: conch chowder, conch fritters and cracked conch. All are made from the meat of the gastropods that lend the name "Conchs" to Keys natives (see "The Conch Republic," page 110). However it's prepared, conch is delicious, if slightly chewy. Key lime pie, made with small, tart round limes native to the Keys, is another culinary specialty that should not be missed.

Shopping

If you're looking for large malls with national brand-name stores, plan on doing your shopping in Miami or Fort Lauderdale at the beginning or end of your trip. The Keys have a lot to offer, though, especially if you want souvenirs and locally crafted gifts or jewelry. Shops selling T-shirts and inexpensive souvenirs have blossomed in Key West to service the daily flood of cruise ship passengers, but the original art galleries and fine jewelry stores are still there too.

The Keys are also a good source for watersports equipment. Several dive outlet stores and some dive shops carry large inventories at low prices. The outlets carry a variety of brands, while the product line in individual dive shops tends to be more brand selective.

Souvenir shops selling coral and seashells were among the first stores to crop up along the Overseas Highway. In the 1950s their inventory was ripped right from the Florida Keys reefs. That's no longer the case, but many shell stores are still doing a booming business, and the shells and coral they do offer come from countries where the environment is not protected. Coral reefs worldwide need our support, so does it make sense to enjoy the reefs here and buy souvenirs from another reef?

Souvenir stands line Key West's Mallory Square.

Activities & Attractions

Most visitors to the Florida Keys are not divers. They come for the myriad other activities and attractions that make the region so appealing, including fishing, sailing, windsurfing, kayaking and, of course, relaxing, shopping and sightseeing. The islands, particularly Key West, are rich in historical attractions and festivals, in addition to a wide variety of outdoor, water-related activities. With a few notable exceptions, advance reservations are unnecessary. If you have your heart set on deep-sea fishing on Tuesday morning and kayaking on Wednesday afternoon, though, calling ahead may be a good idea. Whatever your interests, there is plenty to do after diving.

Glass-Bottom Boats

Ever wish you could share the wonder of exploring a coral reef with your nondiver friends or relatives? A glass-bottom boat trip may be the perfect solution. Available at many locations in the Keys, glass-bottom boats offer those who are unable or unwilling to dive a chance to see the reefs. Most glass-bottom boat trips take about two hours, spending 45 minutes or so on the reef. A trained guide provides expert commentary, explaining the history and ecology of the Keys and introducing all the creatures that pass beneath the boat.

Kayaking & Canoeing

You can rent kayaks and canoes by the hour or the day and go out by yourself or take a guided tour. Mangrove lagoons on either side of the highway are perfect for paddling and present a great alternative when you need a break or high winds make diving uncomfortable. Both sit-on-top and sit-inside kayaks

Kayaks let you explore the shallow mangrove lagoons.

27

are available, suiting a variety of experience levels. Operators will boat you and your kayak to backcountry wilderness areas or trek down to pristine spots in the Dry Tortugas. John Pennekamp Coral Reef State Park sets aside special areas exclusively for canoes and kayaks.

Parasailing

The bird's-eye view of the reef from a parasail is stunning, and the ride is exhilarating. Equipment and techniques have evolved significantly since parasailing was first introduced, improving both safety and convenience. Seated in a specially designed harness, parasailors now take off and land directly from a platform on the boat. Some operators are even able to take two riders at once.

Dolphin Encounters

Chances of seeing dolphins from a boat in the Keys are good. You may see the dorsal fins of a small pod as they cross your wake, or they may actually surf the boat's bow wave. Underwater encounters, however, are rare. If you see dolphins while diving, count yourself among the lucky.

Swimming with one is possible, though, at several facilities that care for captive dolphins. The National Marine Fisheries Service oversees the operation of these facilities to ensure the health and well-being of the dolphins. Depending on the program, encounters may involve observing the dolphins from land, interacting with them from a dock or actually swimming with them in an enclosed area. An introduction to dolphin biology and natural history is included.

PHOTO TAKEN AT DOLPHIN RESEARCH CENTER, GRASSY KEY

Controlled encounters with social Atlantic bottlenose dolphins are very popular.

Advance reservations are required, as participation is limited and these programs are extremely popular.

In the Swim

Facilities in the Keys offering dolphin encounters:

Dolphins Cove
MM 101.9
Key Largo
toll free ☎ 877-365-2683
☎ 305-451-4060
www.dolphinscove.com

Dolphins Plus
31 Corrine Place
Key Largo
☎ 305-451-1993
www.dolphinsplus.com

Dolphin Research Center
MM 59
Grassy Key
☎ 305-289-1121
www.dolphins.org

Theater of the Sea
MM 84.5
Islamorada, Upper Matecumbe Key
☎ 305-664-2431
www.theaterofthesea.com

Fishing

Next to diving, fishing is the most popular activity in the Keys. Many fishers would argue it's the other way around. If you want to wet a line, there are basically three ways to go about it.

You can hire a backcountry guide, complete with flatboat and pole, and try your luck with the bonefish, tarpon and permits in the shallows of Florida Bay. You can join the fun with a couple of dozen other anglers on a party boat and bottom fish along the reef line for yellowtail, groupers and dolphinfish. Or, you can charter a sportfishing boat for a half or whole day and head for deeper water to troll for almost anything that swims.

For more information on fishing, contact the Florida Keys Chambers of Commerce (see Listings, page 139).

Charters leave at dawn from marinas throughout the Keys.

Sailing

If you can demonstrate prior experience and/or certification, there are sailboats for charter at marinas in Miami and near the Keys' population centers. Prices depend on the size of the boat, the season and whether or not you want a crew.

Smaller sailboats, catamarans and sailboards are available throughout the Keys, chiefly on the bayside. Aside from a summer lull in the trade winds, conditions are excellent. The small bays offer shelter from high waves, but allow enough wind for spirited sailing. Most concessionaires also provide basic lessons.

Take a boat out and snorkel the reefs at your pace.

Florida State Parks & Recreation Areas

John Pennekamp Coral Reef State Park is legendary among divers, but it's only part of the state park system in the Keys. A total of 10 parks (see Listings, pages 138-139) offer a wide variety of recreational and educational experiences, from the fossils at **Windley Key** to the **Bahia Honda**'s famous beaches. The parks are normally open from 8am until sunset every day, and entry fees are nominal.

Key West Aquarium

First opened in 1934, the aquarium (1 Whitehead St., ☎ 305-296-2051) features guided tours, shark petting and touch tanks. The 50,000-gallon (190,000-liter) Atlantic Shores Exhibit encompasses the coral reef ecosystem, from mangroves to nearshore reefs. The aquarium is at Mallory Square and is open daily from 10am to 6pm.

Maritime Museums

Loaded with gold, silver and precious jewels, the Spanish galleon *Nuestra Señora de Atocha* was sunk by a hurricane in the Marquesas Keys in 1622. In 1733 a fleet of 21 Spanish galleons loaded with more treasure looted from the New World left Havana for Spain. All but one of the vessels were destroyed by a hurricane in the Upper Keys. Treasure hunter Art McKee found the remains of the fleet and its treasure in the 1950s, and treasure hunter Mel Fisher finally discovered the *Atocha* in 1985.

Many of the artifacts recovered from these wrecks are now on display at maritime museums in Key West, including the **Mel Fisher Maritime Heritage Society Museum** (200 Greene St., ☎ 305-294-2633), the **Key West Shipwreck Historeum** (1 Whitehead St., ☎ 305-292-8990) and the **Wrecker's Museum** (322 Duval St., ☎ 305-294-9504). Other worthwhile maritime collections are on display at the **Key West Lighthouse Museum** (938 Whitehead St., ☎ 305-294-0012), **East Martello Museum & Gallery** (3501 S. Roosevelt Blvd., ☎ 305-296-3913) and **Key West Museum of Art & History** (281 Front St., ☎ 305-295-6616). In Islamorada, **Somewhere in Time** (MM 82, ☎ 305-664-9699) displays and sells historic shipwreck coins, jewelry and artifacts.

Sunset Celebration

Sunsets are more than just solar events in the Keys. As the sun goes down, tourists and locals alike gather to celebrate the end of another day. At **Mallory Square** in Key West, every sunset sparks a festival. Street performers, food vendors and craftspeople join throngs of spectators to witness the fantastic display of light and color on the horizon. Even the cruise ships have to vacate the dock in time to allow a clear view

The splashy sunset celebration at Mallory Square is a long-standing tourist tradition.

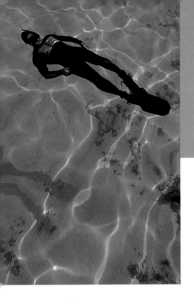

Diving Health & Safety

The Florida Keys are generally a safe place to travel and dive. There are no prevalent diseases, and the water is safe to drink. For most foreign visitors no immunizations are required, though cholera and yellow fever vaccinations may be required of travelers from areas with a history of those diseases. There are medical facilities in the Upper, Middle and Lower Keys, and several major medical institutions are based in Miami.

Sunburn is the most common ailment suffered by visitors, so a good sunscreen is essential. Use a waterproof brand with a minimum SPF of 15. Cover up, seek shade whenever possible and reapply sunscreen frequently, even on overcast days. Dehydration and heat exhaustion can also be a problem in Florida's hot, humid climate, unless you stay properly hydrated. Drink plenty of fluids, especially water or an electrolyte replacement drink. This precaution is particularly important for divers, as dehydration can be a contributing factor in decompression sickness.

Residents joke that the state bird should be the mosquito. The truth is that Florida has about 70 types of mosquitoes and other biting insects such as sand flies and no-see-ums (biting midges). Aerial spraying keeps their numbers in check, but remember to bring plenty of insect repellent. Aloe vera grows wild in Florida and is effective for treating the pain. Just break a leaf off the plant, snap it in half and rub the juice on bites. Over-the-counter medications include calamine lotion, cortisone cream, antihistamines and Tiger Balm, all of which control the itching to varying degrees.

Diving & Flying

Many divers in the Florida Keys arrive by plane. While it's fine to dive soon *after* flying, it's important to remember that your last dive should be completed at least 24 hours *before* your flight to minimize the risk of decompression sickness, caused by residual nitrogen in the blood.

Pre-Trip Preparation

Your general state of health, diving skill level and specific equipment needs are the three most important factors that impact any dive trip. If you honestly assess these before you leave, you'll be well on your way to assuring a safe dive trip.

First, if you're not in shape, start exercising. Second, if you haven't dived for a while (six months is too long), and your skills are rusty, do a local dive with an experienced buddy or take a scuba review course. Feeling good physically

Tips for Evaluating a Dive Boat

Most reefs in the Florida Keys are four to six miles offshore, so dive boat rides average between 20 and 40 minutes. Operators with boats on the bayside may average slightly longer travel times. Time and fuel capacity limit an operator's range, so try to find one fairly close to the reefs you want to dive.

The quality of dive boats in the Keys is exceptionally high for two reasons: U.S. Coast Guard requirements and competition among dive operators. Boats fall into two categories: "six-pack" boats, which are licensed to carry a maximum of six passengers, and "inspected" boats, which are licensed for a specific number of passengers according to their size and design. Both types must be equipped with two-way radios and carry certain emergency equipment, including life jackets. Inspected boats must pass periodic inspections and meet special Coast Guard design parameters; six-pack boats do not. Captains must remain aboard at all times; inspected boats must have at least one additional crew member.

The advantages of a smaller dive boat include more intimate, manageable dive groups, shorter rides when sea conditions are favorable, and flexibility in choosing dive sites. Disadvantages may include bumpy rides in rough conditions and fewer amenities such as marine heads (toilets) and freshwater showers. Advantages of larger boats include riding comfort, marine heads, showers, large camera-rinse barrels and large dive platforms and ladders. The main disadvantage, of course, is the herd of fellow divers.

Stepping off and climbing back aboard can be the most difficult part of a dive, especially if the seas are up. Does the boat have sufficient handholds for you to steady yourself on the dive platform? Is the platform wide and uncluttered? Check the dive ladders, too. They should have solid rungs and reach at least three steps into the water. Ladders angled like stairs are easier to negotiate than vertical ladders.

Since you're going to spend an hour or two aboard the boat, you may as well be comfortable. Does the boat have a selection of seating in and out of the sun? Backrests? Padded seats? Is there drinking water, a cooler with ice for your food and beverages, a freshwater rinse for cameras and gear, an on-deck shower, a marine head?

Finally, and most important, does the boat carry oxygen for treating dive emergencies? Is it enough to keep at least one diver on pure oxygen continuously until the boat reaches land?

and diving regularly will make you a safer diver and enhance your enjoyment underwater.

At least a month before your trip, inspect your dive gear. Remember, your regulator should be serviced annually, whether you've used it or not. If you use a dive computer and can replace the battery yourself, change it before the trip or buy a spare one to take along. Otherwise, send the computer to the manufacturer for a battery replacement.

If possible, find out if the dive center you'll be using rents or services the type of gear you own. If not, you might want to take spare parts or even spare gear. A spare mask is always a good idea.

Purchase any additional equipment you might need, such as a dive light and tank marker light for night diving, a line reel for wreck diving, etc. Make sure you have at least a whistle attached to your BC. Better yet, add a marker tube (also known as a safety sausage or come-to-me).

About a week before taking off, do a final check of your gear, grease o-rings, check batteries and assemble a save-a-dive kit. This kit should at minimum contain spare mask and fin straps, snorkel keeper, mouthpiece, valve cap, zip ties and o-rings. Don't forget to pack a first-aid kit and any necessary medications such as decongestants, ear drops, antihistamines and motion sickness tablets.

A safety sausage makes you visible from the boat.

DAN

Divers Alert Network (DAN) is an international membership association of individuals and organizations sharing a common interest in diving and safety. It operates a 24-hour diving emergency hot line in the U.S.: ☎ **919-684-8111 or 919-684-4DAN** (-4326). The latter accepts collect calls in a dive emergency. Though DAN does not directly provide medical care, it does provide advice on early treatment, evacuation and hyperbaric treatment of diving-related injuries. Divers should contact DAN for assistance as soon as a diving emergency is suspected.

DAN membership is reasonably priced and includes DAN TravelAssist, a membership benefit that covers medical air evacuation from anywhere in the world for any illness or injury. For a small additional fee, divers can get secondary insurance coverage for decompression illness. For membership details, contact DAN at ☎ 800-446-2671 in the U.S. or ☎ 919-684-2948 elsewhere. DAN can also be reached at www.diversalertnetwork.org.

Medical & Recompression Facilities

The Hyperbaric & Problem Wound Center at Mercy Hospital in Miami is DAN's regional coordinator for Florida and the Caribbean. The center has a professionally trained staff and operates two multilock chambers (12- and two-person). A physician trained in hyperbaric medicine and at least two registered nurses are present during all treatments.

The only hospital-based hyperbaric chamber in the Florida Keys is at Mariners Hospital in Tavernier, an affiliate of Baptist Health Systems of South Florida. Seven specially-trained physicians are on call 24 hours a day at its Hyperbaric Medicine Department, along with 20 nurses and respiratory therapists.

Medical Contacts

Hyperbaric Chambers

Mercy Hospital
Hyperbaric & Problem Wound Center
3663 S. Miami Ave.
Miami
Emergency hot line (24 hours)
    ☎ 800-662-3637
    ☎ 305-854-0300

Mariners Hospital
Hyperbaric Medicine Department
MM 91.5
Tavernier, Key Largo
Emergency hot line (24 hours)
    ☎ 305-853-1600
    ☎ 305-853-1603

Hospitals

Upper Keys
Mariners Hospital
MM 91.5
Tavernier, Key Largo
☎ 305-852-4418

Middle Keys
Fishermen's Hospital
MM 48.7
Marathon, Vaca Key
☎ 305-743-5533

Lower Keys
Lower Keys Medical Center
MM 5
5900 College Road
Key West
☎ 305-294-5531

Diving in the Florida Keys

Occasionally you hear someone grouse, "Diving was better in the Keys 30 years ago." Have things changed in three decades? Certainly. Ships run aground, storms take their toll, divers leave careless footprints, and all of us contribute daily to the ecological burden. Even though we would like these reefs to stay the same forever, change is a fact of life. As some areas reach their peak and start to decline, others develop toward their prime.

Are the Keys still a great place to dive? Absolutely. The progress made by Monroe County and the state of Florida toward preserving coastland and curbing pollution, and the protective provisions of the Florida Keys National Marine Sanctuary, have made a difference. Marine life is thriving—diverse in species and abundant in sheer numbers.

Depths at the most popular reef sites range between 5 and 40ft (2 and 12m), and water temperatures are comfortable year-round (see Climate, page 18), allowing for plenty of bottom time. The dramatic thermoclines found in northern latitudes are not present in the Florida Keys, so water temperatures change little with depth.

Visibility is normally in the 40 to 70ft (12 to 21m) range on the outer reefs, but it can vary greatly by location and weather conditions. Generally speaking, the outer reefs offer better visibility than the inner reefs. Visibility drops both during and after storms, though it recovers quickly. Calm conditions from late spring through autumn mean more high-visibility days than during the windy winter. Stunning days of 100ft (30m) visibility still occur regularly, so bring your good luck charm and hope the weather is on your side.

In the Upper Keys visibility is driven less by tidal action and more by wind strength and position of the Gulf Stream. When winds are relatively calm and the Gulf Stream is closer to Florida than The Bahamas, the Upper Keys will have long periods of high visibility. One major contributing factor is the long, solid mass of Key Largo, which effectively separates the nutrient-laden Florida Bay waters from the warm, clear Atlantic waters.

In the Middle and Lower Keys, open passages between the islands allow Florida Bay and Atlantic waters to mix more readily, so visibility is closely associated with the tides. If visibility is down, it should improve rapidly as the tide comes in.

Water color is often a good indicator of visibility. Wherever blue water is reported, you know visibility will be good. Green water can be clear, but it generally holds more suspended particles.

Currents vary from none at all to very strong, but are generally mild on the shallow reefs. The meaner currents are usually found on the deep reefs or wrecks and are associated with eddies, or countercurrents, in the Gulf Stream. Tidal currents can be very strong in the Marquesas Keys.

Due to the combination of shallow reefs and relatively little protection from the wind, strong surge can sometimes develop here, though it's not normally a problem. If the wind is up, a slight to moderate surge may stir the surface down to about 20ft (6m), especially on the outer reefs.

As the reefs are generally 4 to 6 miles (6 to 10km) offshore, virtually all diving in the Florida Keys is done by boat. See Listings (pages 132-137) for more information on local dive operators.

Reef Terminology

Navigating above and below water is simpler if you know a bit about the structure of Florida Keys reefs. The term back reef refers to the landward side of the reef, a relatively stable area of sand and seagrass that is usually 3 to 10ft (1 to 3m) deep. The reef crest is the shallowest portion of the reef, often exposed at low tide. Imme-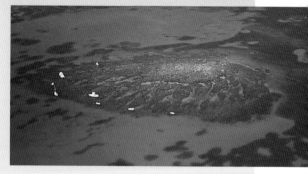diately seaward of the reef crest is an unstable area called the rubble zone, where small bits of gray, fossilized coral are deposited by wave action. Most diving takes place on the fore reef, an extensive area between 10 and 35ft (3 and 11m) deep.

The fore reef is composed of parallel ridges of coral separated by narrow sand channels, commonly referred to as a spur-and-groove formation. The spurs are topped with coral polyps and sponges, but their structure is composed of calcium carbonate deposited over the millennia by ancestors of the living corals. When you cross the spurs, you're going parallel to shore. Swimming along the spurs will take you either toward land and shallower water or seaward into deeper water.

At the seaward end of the spurs, the reef flattens out into the intermediate reef, an area of abundant soft corals. The deep reef slopes from about 45ft (14m) to between 60 and 90ft (18 and 27m), where the flat, sandy bottom begins. A lower profile spur-and-groove formation is often present, with large soft-coral colonies and many sponges among the scattered hard corals.

Dive Training & Certification

Many people learn to dive in the Florida Keys, or take the written portion of the certification course at home and come to the Keys on a referral for the Open Water dives. The spectrum of certifying agencies—PADI, NAUI, SSI, BSAC, YMCA and others—are represented, and the large number of qualified instructors often allows students to select their instructor by gender, language spoken, etc.

Many divers take additional training here too, from Advanced Open Water to Instructor and beyond. Most specialty courses are also available, including Wreck Diver, Underwater Photographer and Underwater Naturalist. Classes can be arranged to fit nearly any schedule.

Snorkeling

Snorkeling is not just something to do till you learn how to scuba dive—in itself it's a great way to see the reefs, and it's loads of fun. Great snorkeling sites abound in the Keys. Many reefs and wrecks have extensive shallow sections within 10ft (3m) of the surface. Even if you simply float in place, you'll see plenty of healthy hard and soft corals and dozens of reef fish species. Long swims are not required, since moorings are often right on top of the best snorkeling sites.

Especially while snorkeling, remember to cover up to avoid sunburn. A lycra dive skin or T-shirt, plus a generous coating of waterproof sunscreen, will protect your skin.

If you're new to the sport, here are a few tips:

- Check the fit. Most masks will fit most people, but not always. Without using the strap, put the mask to your face and inhale through your nose. The suction should hold the mask to your face.
- Clean the lens. Silicone from the manufacturing process leaves a film that will fog up the mask until you scrub it off with a mild abrasive cleanser. Toothpaste works great—use it on both sides and the skirt the first time. A dab swirled around the inside of the glass before every use should keep it fog free. Anti-fogging drops are available, though the old standby, saliva (yes, spit), also works perfectly well. To protect your eyes, rinse the mask thoroughly before using.
- If you have trouble breathing through a snorkel, try this simple procedure before you leave the dock: Relax, put the snorkel in your mouth when you're ready and breathe for a few minutes. You'll adjust to the feeling and be more comfortable when you hop in the water.
- Use a snorkel with a purge valve. These one-way valves allow you to expel water from the snorkel by blowing gently into the mouthpiece or simply breathing normally. You won't have to take the snorkel out of your mouth or raise your head out of the water.
- If you're unsure of your snorkeling skills, wear a flotation vest and stay near the boat. You'll see lots of fish even if you hold onto the dive ladder. When you gain confidence, explore the reef.
- Please don't stand on the coral—you'll be killing coral polyps if you do.

Water safety training begins in childhood.

Live-Aboards

Live-aboards are unnecessary throughout most of the Keys, as the reefs are easily accessed by shore-based dive centers. Two charter boats do operate as live-aboards in the Lower Keys, however. Based out of Key West, both offer custom itineraries to the remote reefs of the Marquesas Keys and Dry Tortugas. (See Listings, page 138, for contact information.)

Dive Site Icons

The symbols at the beginning of each dive site description provide a quick summary of some of the following characteristics present at each site:

 Good snorkeling or free-diving site.

 Remains or partial remains of a wreck can be seen at this site.

 Sheer wall or drop-off.

 Deep dive. Features of this dive occur in water deeper than 90ft (27m).

 Strong currents may be encountered at this site.

 Strong surge (the horizontal movement of water caused by waves) may be encountered at this site.

 Drift dive. Because of strong currents and/or difficulty in anchoring, a drift dive is recommended at this site.

 Beach/shore dive. This site can be accessed from shore.

 Poor visibility. The site often has visibility of less than 40ft (12m).

 Caves are a prominent feature of this site. Only experienced cave divers should explore inner cave areas.

 Marine preserve. Special regulations apply in this area.

Pisces Rating System for Dives & Divers

The dive sites in this book are rated according to the following diver skill-level rating system. These are not absolute ratings but apply to divers at a particular time, diving at a particular place. For instance, someone unfamiliar with prevailing conditions might be considered a novice diver at one dive area, but an intermediate diver at another, more familiar location.

Novice: A novice diver should be accompanied by an instructor, divemaster or advanced diver on all dives. A novice diver generally fits the following profile:
◆ basic scuba certification from an internationally recognized certifying agency
◆ dives infrequently (less than one trip a year)
◆ logged fewer than 25 total dives
◆ little or no experience diving in similar waters and conditions
◆ dives no deeper than 60ft (18m)

Intermediate: An intermediate diver generally fits the following profile:
◆ may have participated in some form of continuing diver education
◆ logged between 25 and 100 dives
◆ dives no deeper than 130ft (40m)
◆ has been diving in similar waters and conditions within the last six months

Advanced: An advanced diver generally fits the following profile:
◆ advanced certification
◆ has been diving for more than two years and logged over 100 dives
◆ has been diving in similar waters and conditions within the last six months

Regardless of your skill level, you should be in good physical condition and know your limitations. If you are uncertain of your own level of expertise for a particular site, ask the advice of a local dive instructor. He or she is best qualified to assess your abilities based on the site's prevailing dive conditions. Ultimately, however, you must decide if you are capable of making a particular dive, a decision that should take into account your level of training, recent experience and physical condition, as well as the conditions at the site. Remember that conditions can change at any time, even during a dive.

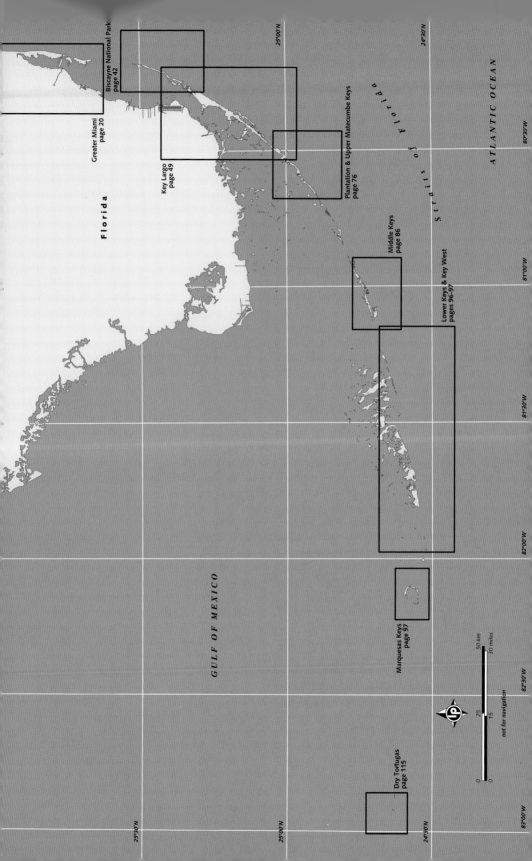

Biscayne National Park Dive Sites

Most visitors to the Florida Keys take Florida's Turnpike south from Miami, which feeds them onto the Overseas Highway (U.S. 1) about midway down the island of Key Largo. It's easy to skip right past Biscayne National Park and the reefs between Miami and Key Largo, as accessibility is somewhat limited.

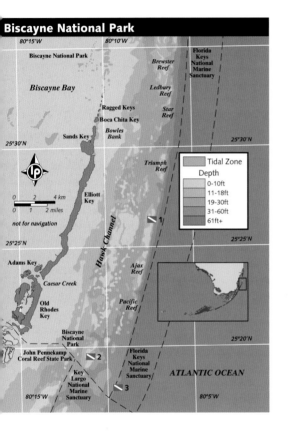

The Biscayne National Park visitor's center at Convoy Point is a short drive from the turnpike extension, but it's a boater's park from there on out. Private boats generally cruise down from the Miami area. The park includes most of Biscayne Bay and the string of undeveloped islands—including Boca Chita, Elliott and Adams Keys—between Miami and the Upper Keys. The concessionaire at Convoy Point can take you to Elliott Key for a bit of exploring or out to the reefs for diving and snorkeling. Live coral cover tapers off the farther north you go, but many nice dive sites lie within the park.

The infamous pirate Black Caesar used these islands as a base in the early 1800s, entering the bay via Caesar Creek south of Elliott Key. The iron ring on Caesar Rock is where he supposedly tied a line to the top of his mast to pull his ship nearly over on its side. Hidden from view, but fully

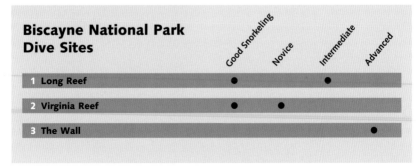

42

rigged and ready to go, Caesar would wait until a passing ship was close by, then release the line and charge out of the creek to overtake his victim.

Other attractions south of Miami include the Weeks Air Museum at Kendall-Tamiami Airport, the Metrozoo on SW 152nd Street, the Monkey Jungle on SW 216th Street, the Parrot Jungle & Gardens on SW 57th Avenue and the Metro-Dade Homestead Motorsports Complex, which hosts NASCAR, SCCA and CART races on an oval track and an infield road course. The Everglades Alligator Farm, Gator Park and the Coral Castle are just a few miles farther south, near the entrance to Everglades National Park, which is just off the turnpike extension in Florida City. Fresh water flows from the Everglades to Florida Bay and onto the reefs, and the hydrological balance of this "river of grass" is crucial to the overall health of the Florida Keys ecosystem.

Aerial look at the Everglades.

1 Long Reef

About midway between the lights of Triumph and Pacific Reefs, Long Reef stretches for nearly 2 miles, a hazardous shallow trap for the unwary mariner. The reef has claimed many victims over the years, including the ships *Lugana*, *Alicia* and *Mandalay*. Divers and snorkelers can explore all three wrecks.

The steamship *Lugana* is an early 1900s steel freighter. Most of the hull has been reduced to twisted metal, but the boiler is still easy to find. *Alicia* was a 345ft steamship built in 1883. She ran aground on Long Reef in 1905, and her scattered remains lie in 20ft of water. *Mandalay* is a 128ft steel schooner resting in only 10ft of water.

The reef crest at Long Reef is about 3ft deep at its shallowest point and is divided near the middle by a prominent cut. The fore reef slopes down steadily from 10ft to around 30ft, then transitions into

Location: 6 nautical miles (11km) NE of Caesar Creek

Depth Range: Surface-60ft (18m)

Access: Boat

Expertise Rating: Intermediate

a flatter profile and milder slope until 55 or 60ft, where it levels off on a sandy plain. Expect to see lots of damselfish, including sergeant majors, bicolor damselfish and brown chromis. Parrotfish are also plentiful, especially stoplight and princess parrotfish. Parrotfish go through several distinct phases during their lives. Smaller juveniles look considerably different than the adults, particularly the sexually mature supermales, the largest and most familiar phase.

2 Virginia Reef

This reef is typical of many shallow dive sites in Biscayne National Park. Only about 8ft deep at the shallowest sections and 20ft deep around the perimeter, it's suitable for both snorkeling and scuba diving. The reef structure is a sprawling calcium carbonate dome scattered with small to medium-sized mounds of hard coral and topped with colonies of elkhorn

Location: 4 nautical miles (7.6km) SE of Caesar Creek

Depth Range: 8-20ft (2-6m)

Access: Boat

Expertise Rating: Novice

Fragile stands of elkhorn coral thrive in the shallows.

coral. The fast-growing elkhorn takes a beating occasionally from tropical storms, but recovers quickly during kinder years when storms spare the Keys.

The sides of the reef taper down into pockets of flat sand. The herbivorous fish living here quickly devour any sea-grass within 80 to 100ft of the reef, but outside of this halo, patches of turtle grass grow like lawns. Their deep root systems stabilize the bottom, and their wide blades trap sediment, helping to preserve water clarity on the reef.

The sand pockets are not deserts, however. Southern stingrays camouflage themselves beneath a light coat of sand or feed on the thousands of invertebrates that burrow in it. Higher on the reef, the fish weave a living tapestry of color. Red squirrelfish hug the reef, blue and yellow queen angelfish skim over it and purple creole wrasses swim above it. You'll spot dozens more species on a single visit, and first-timers will need a fish ID guide to sort them all out.

3 | The Wall

Towering vertical walls, like those found in The Bahamas and the Cayman Islands, are not part of the underwater topography of the Florida Keys. The word *wall* is used in a number of popular dive site names, but the only two that come close to true wall stature are Conch Wall off Key Largo and this one off Key Biscayne. Dives at The Wall are generally conducted as drift dives, since the current may be quite strong.

A fairly level reeftop forms the top edge of the wall, an area of hard bottom covered primarily by tall gorgonians and isolated mounds of star coral or domes of mustard hill coral. Barrel sponges grow in clusters, as large as old oak stumps. The top of the wall runs between 60 and 70ft deep and drops off precipitously to the flat sandy bottom at about 105ft. Scattered coral heads extend out along the sand, but limited bottom

Location: 6 nautical miles (11km) SE of Caesar Creek

Depth Range: 60-105ft (18-32m)

Access: Boat

Expertise Rating: Advanced

time may preclude exploring very far from the wall.

More barrel sponges cling to the side of the wall, along with the thick lattices of deepwater sea fans. Several shallow grottoes pepper the face of the wall, creating pockets of attraction for marine life. A green moray eel may find temporary shelter there on one dive; a big spiny lobster may claim it the next. Cross back over the top of the wall to see more of the reef before ascending for your safety stop.

Divers can't resist a peek inside leathery barrel sponges that grow at depth along the wall.

Upper Keys Dive Sites

The longest island in the Florida Keys, Key Largo stretches about 33 miles (53km), separating the Atlantic Ocean from Florida Bay. Since the warm, clear waters of the ocean are better for coral reef development than the cooler, more nutrient-rich bay waters, the Atlantic reefs benefit from better growing conditions. The result is a long string of highly developed coral reefs paralleling Key Largo's southeastern shore. All the Upper Keys reefs are within the Florida Keys National Marine Sanctuary, which abuts Biscayne National Park and extends protection of the reefs to the Dry Tortugas.

Prior to the arrival of European explorers in the early 1500s, Key Largo was part of the territory controlled by the Calusa Indians, whose settlements extended outward from the Tampa Bay area. At the time, the land was covered with hardwoods, including many superb giant mahogany trees. Settlers later stripped most of the prized mahogany, and Key Largo became briefly known for its Key limes and pineapples. Now the orchards are gone too, though the northern half of the island is still largely undeveloped, except for the private Ocean Reef Club.

State Road 905 runs up this half of Key Largo, providing an alternate route off the island. Crocodile Lake National Wildlife Refuge, a protected habitat of the American crocodile, occupies much of the land on the west side of the road. The state of Florida acquired most of the land on the east side of the road, now protected as a botanical site.

Just after U.S. 1 crosses Jewfish Creek and Lake Surprise, it joins State Road 905 and becomes the Overseas Highway. From this point, driving south along the Overseas Highway will bring you past all the dive shops, restaurants, hotels, stores and attractions in the Upper Keys.

Fishing has been a Keys mainstay over the years, especially on Plantation, Windley and Upper and Lower Matecumbe Keys, an area collectively known as Islamorada (pronounced eye-luh-murr-AH-da). In fact, Islamorada is known as the "Sportfishing Capital of the World," for its combination of deep-sea fishing in the Atlantic and backcountry fishing on the Florida Bay flats. The fish camps of old have evolved into resorts and marinas that still promise world-class fishing.

Key West doesn't hold the patent on spectacular sunsets.

Key Largo

Often confusing to Upper Keys visitors is that Key Largo is the name of both the island and the unincorporated town that extends from about MM 97 north of MM 106. Prior to 1952 the town was called Rock Harbor, but that now refers only to the small community at the south end of town. At the north end of town is Garden Cove, a community that dates back to the late 1800s, when the Carysfort Lighthouse keepers maintained a vegetable garden on the site.

As you might expect, since the greatest concentration of dive sites is off Key Largo, the bulk of the Keys' dive shops are also on the island. Dive shops and boats are along both sides of the highway. Near the center of activity is the entrance to John Pennekamp Coral Reef State Park, at MM 102.5. The park grounds include a camping area, visitor's center, a small beach, nature trails and the concessionaire's boats. Another concentration of shops, boats, hotels and stores clusters around MM 100. The next enclave of shops is at the south end of the island in the town of Tavernier (prounounced ta-ver-NEER). The only movie theater in the Upper Keys is in the shopping center at Tavernier.

Other attractions on Key Largo include Jules' Undersea Lodge at the Key Largo Undersea Park (MM 103.2), Dolphin Cove (MM 101.9), the *African Queen,* from the Humphrey Bogart and Katherine Hepburn movie (MM 100), Dolphins Plus (MM 99.5), the Wild Bird Rehabilitation Center (MM 93.6) and Harry Harris Park & Beach (MM 92.5).

Christ of the Deep witnesses an underwater wedding at Key Largo Dry Rocks.

Key Largo Dive Sites

	Good Snorkeling	Novice	Intermediate	Advanced
4 Turtle Rocks	●	●		
5 Carysfort Reef	●		●	
6 South Carysfort Reef	●		●	
7 Civil War Wreck		●		
8 *City of Washington*	●	●		
9 The Elbow	●		●	
10 Horseshoe Reef	●	●		
11 North North Dry Rocks	●	●		
12 North Dry Rocks	●	●		
13 Key Largo Dry Rocks	●	●		
14 Grecian Rocks (Fore Reef)	●	●		
15 Grecian Rocks (Back Reef)	●	●		
16 *Spiegel Grove*				●
17 *Benwood*	●	●		
18 French Reef	●		●	
19 White Bank (North & South)	●	●		
20 Three Sisters	●	●		
21 Sand Island	●		●	
22 Molasses Reef (North End)	●		●	
23 Molasses Reef (Deep)				●
24 Molasses Reef (South End)	●		●	
25 *Bibb*				●
26 *Duane*				●
27 Pickles	●		●	

4　Turtle Rocks

The name Turtle Rocks refers to the shallow reef that extends generally north and south for about a mile and a half opposite Angelfish Creek and the Ocean Reef Club. You may also hear it called Turtle Reef, which is actually the north end of the reef. The bottom surrounding the reef is 25 to 30ft deep, and a channel runs along its west side, flanked by the rectangular green Nos. 1, 3 and 5 markers. Mooring buoys are in place on both sides of the reef, but the best diving is along its east side. The buoys to the west are used primarily by fishers.

Location: 4 nautical miles (7.6km) SE of Ocean Reef Harbor

Depth Range: Surface-30ft (9m)

Access: Boat

Expertise Rating: Novice

The site is composed of a series of patch reefs linked together or growing in close proximity. In the shallowest spots, the coral at Turtle Rocks comes within a foot or two of the surface, but the reef has an interesting up-and-down profile with lots of shelter for fish. The bottom of the reef is pocked with small ravines and natural indentations that are worth exploring. Its position almost 2 nautical miles from the outer reef line shields the site from wave action and currents,

Turtle Tips

Hawksbill, green and loggerhead turtles are all fairly common in the Keys, and telling one from the other is easy if you know what to look for. Hawksbill turtles (*Eretmochelys imbricata*) have a distinctive beak (see photo), and the slightly overlapping scales along the outer edge of their carapace have a jagged appearance. Green turtles (*Chelonia mydas*) have a smoother look, with a smaller beak and evenly joined scales. Loggerhead turtles (*Caretta caretta*), as their common name suggests, have massive heads compared to the others. Adult loggerheads grow the largest of these three species, weighing up to 350 pounds (160 kg).

All sea turtles breathe air, but they may go several hours between breaths while sleeping or resting. During normal activity, however, they breathe every five minutes or so and may need to breathe more often if stressed. In general, loggerheads eat clams and crustaceans, while hawksbills prefer sponges and green turtles dine on turtle grass and algae.

Aside from the fact that harassing sea turtles is prohibited by the Marine Mammal Protection Act, attempting to handle or ride them is poor diving etiquette. The best way to enjoy an extended, up close encounter is to be patient. Approach the turtle slowly and from an angle rather than straight on. Direct eye contact signals an aggressive intent, so don't lock your eyes on the turtle.

making it a good choice on windy days. Expect visibility to be somewhat limited, though, due to suspended sediments.

Conflicting stories say the reef was named either for turtles seen mating here or for the turtle-like appearance of the shallow coral heads. Either way, hawksbill turtles are frequent visitors, as well as snook, spotted morays and stoplight parrotfish.

5 Carysfort Reef

This reef was named for HMS *Carysford*, a frigate that ran aground here on October 23, 1770, though down through the years the last letter was mistakenly changed from D to T. The ship is one in a long list of vessels that have wrecked on this extensive shallow reef. The danger was so great that a lightship was stationed nearby for many years. The lighthouse was constructed 1852 and still towers 112ft above the reef, sitting on the original screw-pile foundation legs. After years of neglect, the structure was renovated in the late 1990s, with the goal of establishing a research facility directly on the reef.

Mooring buoys on the back reef are in 6 to 8ft of water. The site is in the lee of the reef from the prevailing winds, which come out of the northeast, and the water is normally very calm. Snorkeling is excellent among the scattered coral heads on the sand and along the back edge of the reef. The reeftop is shallow enough to be impassable even for snorkelers at low tide.

Look up while you're in the shallows and you may see slender, almost translucent houndfish skimming along just beneath the surface. Although houndfish often blend in with the waves, these predators are easily identified by their needle-like snouts. The shallows are also a good place to find reef fish that graze on algae, including rainbow and stoplight parrotfish, blue tangs, doctorfish and bicolor damselfish.

Location: 6 nautical miles (11km) SE of Ocean Reef Harbor

Depth Range: Surface-80ft (24m)

Access: Boat

Expertise Rating: Intermediate

Another series of mooring buoys along the east side and southern tip marks the outside of the reef. The depth beneath these buoys ranges from 20 to 30ft. The

The lighthouse gleams after a recent renovation.

reef structure is typical Florida Keys coral spur and sand groove, except the sand patches are not as prominent as at reefs farther south. The ridges here change direction, and the sand channels boast additional coral heads, creating a network of interesting cul-de-sacs and alleyways.

Another unusual feature of Carysfort Reef is the fossil reef formation at 55ft.

A second spur-and-groove formation lies at this depth, the site of an ancient reef that was "drowned" as water levels rose thousands of years ago. This deeper part of the reef features a greater concentration of sponge life than the shallower sections and naturally attracts reef fish that eat sponges, including all of the members of the angelfish family common to the Florida Keys.

6 South Carysfort Reef

The expansive reef crest of South Carysfort Reef is exposed at low tide and is barely deep enough to be crossed by snorkelers at high tide. Watch where you're going and keep an eye on the tide or you could find yourself with a long swim around the reef back to the boat. Much of the reeftop is fossil coral now, due to a series of storms over the last decade, but the elkhorn and staghorn corals are coming back in many spots.

Schools of several dozen midnight parrotfish or several hundred surgeonfish roam amid the coral branches in the shallows. Every few minutes they will stop en masse and munch greedily on the algae or the reef structure itself. At

Location: 6.5 nautical miles (12km) SE of Ocean Reef Harbor

Depth Range: Surface-80ft (24m)

Access: Boat

Expertise Rating: Intermediate

some unseen signal they'll form up again and head off for another part of the reef.

Mooring buoys line both sides of the reef. The back reef buoys are convenient for snorkeling and are more protected when the wind is strong out of the northeast or east. The front reef buoys are good for snorkeling too, but they'll also put you in a good position for scuba diving. The depth near the front buoys is around 30ft, and you can work your way down a gradual slope to 50 or 60ft or head up toward the reef crest. The stretch between the buoys and the reef crest offers many large coral heads and interesting valleys. The corals also form several arches and swim-throughs.

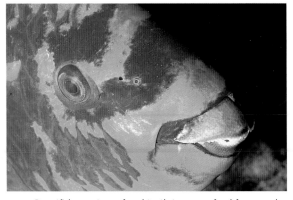
Parrotfish use strong fused teeth to scrape food from corals.

7   Civil War Wreck

Called the Civil War Wreck because it appears to date from around 1860 to 1865, this is a very popular wreck with photographers. It lies on a flat sandy bottom not far from the tower at The Elbow, and the maximum depth is about 20ft. More than a century underwater has reduced the wreck to wood timbers fastened with iron pins.

If you're not into fish-watching or photography, the Civil War Wreck may bore you after 20 minutes, because it's not a particularly large site. On the other hand, the wreck is packed with cottonwicks, dog snappers, Spanish grunts and hundreds of other reef fish. Spotted moray eels and coneys are easy to find, and you can count on a variety of parrotfish and angelfish.

Location: 6 nautical miles (11km) ESE of Garden Cove

Depth Range: 15-20ft (5-6m)

Access: Boat

Expertise Rating: Novice

Corals and sponges grow on every exposed surface of the timbers, creating a rich habitat for invertebrates. This wreck is a good spot to find nudibranchs, anemones, brittle stars and hermit crabs. The structure of the wreck is extremely fragile, so the best place to search is along the edges, where you can keep your knees and fins on the sand.

The wreck's timbers shelter a variety of fish, including mixed schools of grunts and snappers.

8 *City of Washington*

Built by the shipyard of John Roach and Sons in Pennsylvania in 1877, the steamship *City of Washington* was 320ft long with a 38ft beam. In addition to her engines, the ship was fitted with two masts and a full set of sails. For many years the ship carried passengers between New York and Havana, and she was anchored near the battleship USS *Maine* when that ship exploded in Havana Harbor in 1898. The *City of Washington's* crew rescued 90 sailors from the tragedy.

In 1908 her engines were removed, and the ship was converted to a barge. While under tow by the tugboat *Edgar F. Luckenbach*, *City of Washington* struck the reef and sank. The wreckage was later considered a hazard to navigation and was dynamited. The basic hull form is still intact, but the other parts of the

Location: 6 nautical miles (11km) ESE of Garden Cove

Depth Range: 15-25ft (5-8m)

Access: Boat

Expertise Rating: Novice

ship have been reduced to large pieces of metal plate. The maximum depth on the wreck is 25ft.

Great barracuda and green moray eels have been hand-fed at this site for many years, acclimating them to contact with divers. Don't be alarmed if you suddenly find one about 4 inches from your mask, expectantly looking you in the eye. Curl your fingers up so they won't be mistaken for small baitfish, and keep your hands by your sides.

The wreck of the *City of Washington* is a superb night dive. Its shallow depth makes it perfect for the last dive of the day, and navigation is easy because you can just stay on or near the wreck. The marine life you see at night is very different from that seen during the day, as an entirely new cast takes the stage, including spider crabs and brittle stars.

A diver explores the shattered remains of this 19th century steamship.

9   The Elbow

The sparkling clarity of the water in the Florida Keys is due to the Gulf Stream, which regularly sloshes its warm blueness over the reefs. The center of the Gulf Stream wanders a bit between Florida and The Bahamas, though, and the water in the Upper Keys changes with the position of the stream. Nearshore water bathes the reefs in green, the Gulf Stream turns them blue, and a mix will appear blue-green. The Elbow, which juts out into the path of the Gulf Stream slightly more than other reefs, enjoys the benefits of clear blue water more often. When it's green at Carysfort and blue-green at French, it's probably blue on The Elbow. The price for this blue water is the occasional moderate current.

Location: 6 nautical miles (11km) ESE of Garden Cove

Depth Range: 15-85ft (5-26m)

Access: Boat

Expertise Rating: Intermediate

Scattered remains of several wrecks litter the reef, including the *City of Washington*, the Civil War Wreck and the *Tonawanda*, a steamer that sank here in 1866. The depth is about 15ft over the shallowest ridges, which slope in a fairly even gradient toward deep water. The prominent ridges appear to end in 30 to 35ft of water, and the bottom is more uniformly flat, although as you move into deeper water, you'll pick up vestiges of the coral ridges and sand channels. Turtle encounters, mostly with hawksbills and loggerheads, are frequent between 20 and 35ft anywhere on The Elbow.

One deeper mooring buoy sits atop the southern reef section. The depth is just below 50ft at the buoy, and the bottom slopes very gradually toward a lip at 55ft called "Nelson's Ledge." The terrain slopes more steeply from that point, ending with scattered corals on a sand bottom in 85ft. This area is characterized by prolific soft corals, lower-profile star and brain corals, many tube and finger sponges and large numbers of giant barrel sponges. Queen angelfish, blue angelfish and four common Florida species of butterflyfish—spotfin, foureye, banded and reef—are abundant.

Gulf Stream currents bathe this site in blue water.

10 Horseshoe Reef

When the wind has been calm for a day or two, the water clarity on the inside reefs improves. When the calm winds are accompanied by an influx of blue Gulf Stream water, the visibility increases dramatically. Under those circumstances, Horseshoe can be one of the top shallow dives or snorkel sites in the Keys. This is still a nice reef on any day, even if the visibility is reduced.

Location: 4 nautical miles (7.6km) SE of Garden Cove

Depth Range: 8-22ft (2-7m)

Access: Boat

Expertise Rating: Novice

The depth is 8 to 10ft on the reeftop, with a 22ft maximum in the sand on the seaward side. In spite of its name, the reef is a long bank of coral, featuring very large colonies of star, starlet and brain corals along the crest and branching corals on the back reef. A U-shaped sandy hole in the northern section of the reef, which is only apparent from a bird's eye view, may account for the "horseshoe" appellation.

Slightly south of midway along the reef face, 6 to 10ft in from the sand, you'll find the shaft of a large and very old anchor sticking out of the reef. It wears a thick beard of encrusting sponges and soft corals as a disguise, but you'll spot it if you watch for the round shape of the ring at the top of the shaft. There are also curious blocks of pumice scattered along the sand in front of the reef, each a bit larger than a loaf of bread.

In addition to many other species of reef fish, Horseshoe hosts several schools of tiny silversides. During the summer months they swirl around beneath the coral ledges, sometimes in numbers so large they swell out into the open. You'll see the dynamics of schooling behavior at work if you take a few moments to hang motionless in the water and watch predators like black jacks lace into the school. As the jacks zoom in, the school parts almost instantly. For fish in the middle of the pack, there really is safety in numbers.

Clouds of silversides are a welcome sight to hungry snappers and jacks.

11 North North Dry Rocks

The whimsical name is memorable, and so is the assortment of ever-present angelfish. Every angelfish species in the Keys, including yellow-and-black rock beauties as well as queen, blue, gray and French angelfish, munches on the abundant elephant ear and brown clustered tube sponges that line the ledges of this reef. Copper sweepers also frequent the reef, sheltering beneath the overhangs and sometimes circling ceaselessly beneath the flat arms of an elkhorn coral colony.

Only 5 to 8ft deep atop the coral ridges, the reef bottoms out at 25ft in the sand. The ridges here are among the highest profile in the Keys, rising 20ft in some places and creating substantial canyons that will play havoc with your ears if you try to go up and over each one instead of around the end. North North is not a large reef, but it is too big to cover in a single dive. If you explore two or three canyons on a dive, you're probably going about the right pace to enjoy the scenery

Location: 4.5 nautical miles (8.6km) SE of Garden Cove

Depth Range: 5-25ft (2-8m)

Access: Boat

Expertise Rating: Novice

and marine life. If you're looking for little creatures, you probably won't leave the canyon where you enter the water.

The largest individual coral colonies are near the seaward end of the ridges. Some of the star corals (*Montastraea annularis*) are as tall as a diver. Over the years bright yellow and red boring sponges have invaded the structure of these mounds, lifting the edges of living coral like shingles. Macrophotographers will find excellent subjects like saddled or red-lip blennies perched on the coral polyps or peeking out from a convenient hole.

Angelfish flock here for their favorite snacks, especially the bright orange elephant ear sponges.

12 North Dry Rocks

Four prominent coral ridges form the central section of this reef. The two on the north side of the reef are shorter than the southern ridges, and the southernmost ridge terminates in a distinctive hook at the seaward end. Additional coral patches extend to either side of the main ridges.

North Dry Rocks is a very shallow reef, nearly breaking the surface atop the ridges. The maximum depth is about 25ft at the sand bottom. The once-thick elkhorn and staghorn stands in the shallows have thinned out, but there are still some nice colonies. Depending on where the wind holds your boat, these easily damaged corals may be right below the surface, so enter the water with caution.

Like North North Dry Rocks, the coral ridges here have a very high profile, effectively dividing one passage from another unless you swim over the top or around the end. Near the middle of the reef, a large archway called the "Minnow Cave" is often filled to overflowing with silversides (also called glass minnows) during

Location: 4.5 nautical miles (8.6km) SE of Garden Cove

Depth Range: 5-25ft (2-8m)

Access: Boat

Expertise Rating: Novice

the summer months. The seaward ends of the ridges are capped with a magnificent buttress of huge star coral formations.

North Dry Rocks is a good choice for fish-watching or for photographers shooting fish portraits. If you stay motionless over the sand, the fish will parade past your lens, starting with the bold gray angelfish. French angels are also common here, along with stoplight parrotfish, trumpetfish, scrawled filefish and queen angels. Look under the deepest cut ledges and you'll probably find a school of copper sweepers swirling back and forth in the dim light.

Copper sweepers camouflage a pair of spiny lobsters entrenched beneath an overhang.

13 Key Largo Dry Rocks

This site is also simply called The Statue, since the bronze statue known as *Christ of the Deep* stands here, but the reef was originally named Grecian Rocks. On an early chart its name was transposed with that of a nearby reef, and both have had the other's name since then. Both reefs are so shallow that parts of them break the surface at low tide, although it's actually

Location: 4.5 nautical miles (8.6km) SE of Garden Cove

Depth Range: Surface-30ft (9m)

Access: Boat

Expertise Rating: Novice

fossil and living coral that you see, not rocks as the names imply.

Key Largo Dry Rocks is a transition reef, exhibiting characteristics of both patch reefs and outer bank reefs. Like most patch reefs, it's oval in shape with sides that slope to sand. However, the seaward portion of the reef has coral spurs and sandy grooves like the outer reefs. Maximum depth on this side is about 30ft. The back reef features large boulder corals in about 20ft of water. This side of the reef is marked by a diamond-shaped day marker, which warns of shallow water.

You might see any of the fish or invertebrates common to the Keys at this site, merely by swimming slowly along the reef. Many divers ignore the seagrass patches on the sand surrounding the reef, but these are fertile areas too. Majestic helmet conchs and elegantly shaped lightning whelks sometimes cross the flats, along with southern stingrays and a variety of reef fish.

The 9ft statue of Christ is on the seaward side, near a floating spar buoy. The statue is one of at least three cast from a mold by Italian sculptor Guido Galletti. The first, called *Christ of the Abyss*, was placed in 50ft of water off Genoa. A second casting was made in 1961 and presented to the people of Grenada for their assistance in rescuing passengers from a fire aboard the Italian liner *Bianca C.* That statue is on display in St. George's Harbour in Grenada.

This statue, the third casting, was originally made for Egidi Cressi, whose company manufactures dive equipment. Cressi eventually donated the statue to the Underwater Society of America, who in turn passed it to the Florida Board of Parks & Historic Memorials for display. In 1966 Ellison Hardee, the first superintendent of John Pennekamp Coral Reef State Park, organized the effort to install the statue on its massive concrete pedestal at Key Largo Dry Rocks.

14 Grecian Rocks (Fore Reef)

Grecian Rocks is about a mile in from the main reef line and is known as an inner bank reef. The reef profile is an abbreviated version of the spur-and-groove formation so common on the outer reefs. The fore reef is a moderately steep slope, starting near the surface and descending to about 25ft near the mooring buoys on the seaward side. The bottom levels out in flat sand at 28 to 30ft, with scattered clumps of coral trailing away from the reef. Branching corals in the shallows give way to mixed hard and soft corals in the midsection and larger hard corals near the bottom. Fossil coral ridges are exposed in many places, with only a light covering of live coral.

Location: 5 nautical miles (9.5km) SE of Garden Cove

Depth Range: Surface-30ft (9m)

Access: Boat

Expertise Rating: Novice

Grecian Rocks is a sanctuary preservation area, which affords it added protection against damage to corals and seagrass, as well as a prohibition against fishing. The populations of reef and predatory fish on Grecian have grown appreciably since the SPA was designated in July 1997. Expect to see almost any of the common Keys reef fish here.

The mooring buoys wrap around the south side of the reef, where a cut forms a deep pass through the corals. The reef south of the pass is known as **Banana Reef**. Although it is slightly shallower, Banana Reef is similar to Grecian Rocks.

Swim up and Be Counted

Founded in 1990 and based on Key Largo, the Reef Environmental Education Foundation (REEF) is a nonprofit that relies on volunteers to compile a comprehensive database of reef fish populations (a fish census of sorts) for use in marine life management. You can conduct surveys on your own, as part of a group or by joining the annual Great American Fish Count, held each July. REEF membership is free, and learning to conduct a survey is easy. (For example, the glamour puss at right belongs to a honeycomb cowfish.)

REEF HQ and Visitor's Center
MM 106
P.O. Box 246
Key Largo, FL 33037
☎ 305-451-0312 fax: 305-451-0028
www.reef.org

15 Grecian Rocks (Back Reef)

On windy days the back reef at Grecian Rocks is the last refuge of snorkel boats, as the broad, shallow reef provides an excellent lee. On calm days it can still draw a crowd, because it's such a perfect spot for novice divers. The maximum depth behind the reef is 6ft, but much of the site is 4ft or less. The bottom is mostly sand and beds of turtle grass. At the back edge of the reef is a narrow rubble zone beside the coral shelf that delineates the reef crest. Wave action and high visitor impact have reduced the live coral cover on the reef crest, but it's still an interesting area. At low tide parts of the reef may be more than a foot out of the water.

First-time snorkelers are usually captivated by the many colorful reef fish that feed along the reef crest, but the sand and seagrass are also full of life. Queen

Location: 5 nautical miles (9.5km) SE of Garden Cove

Depth Range: Surface-6ft (2m)

Access: Boat

Expertise Rating: Novice

conch are plentiful on the back reef, in addition to hermit crabs, juvenile grunts and snappers, and hundreds of invertebrates. Although the shallow water and sand bottom may tempt you to stand up, please don't, because every bit of the bottom harbors life of some kind.

Little Grecian, an unmarked shallow reef several hundred yards to the north, is a good alternative for snorkeling if the weather is calm. The reef is a flat dome, about 5ft deep on top and perhaps 12ft deep along the outer edges.

Sea fans and other gorgonians are especially numerous amid the smaller hard corals here.

16   *Spiegel Grove*

Named for the Ohio estate of Rutherford B. Hayes, 19th president of the United States, *Spiegel Grove* was built in Pascagoula, Mississippi, by Ingalls Shipbuilding Corp. Launched on June 8, 1956, the ship was designated LSD-32 (landing ship, dock), with a cavernous well deck that could be flooded to launch amphibious craft during a beach assault. The ship could also accommodate hundreds of troops during the journey to a war zone anywhere in the world.

Based in Norfolk, Virginia, *Spiegel Grove* supported military exercises in the Atlantic, Caribbean and Mediterranean, but her greatest service was in welfare, not warfare. In 1961 *Spiegel Grove* carried tons of medical supplies, food, books and

Location: 4.5 nautical miles (8.6km) east of Mosquito Bank light

Depth Range: 40-130ft (12-40m)

Access: Boat

Expertise Rating: Advanced

toys to Africa, visiting Gambia, Zanzibar, Kenya, South Africa and the Seychelles during a four-month goodwill tour. In 1963 the ship embarked on a similar mission, steaming 21,000 miles to visit nine countries.

At 510ft long with an 84ft beam, *Spiegel Grove* will be one of the largest

COURTESY OF U.S. NAVAL INSTITUTE

The *Spiegel Grove* saw duty throughout the world, including goodwill missions to Africa.

When in service, the vast well deck could be flooded to launch amphibious landing craft.

diveable shipwrecks in the world. Her steam turbines produced 24,000 horsepower, giving her a top speed of 24 knots. The well deck, enormous deck cranes, antiaircraft batteries and large superstructure will make this wreck an extremely effective artificial reef. The bottom at the wreck site is between 100 and 130ft.

Expect to see the entire marine food chain represented on the wreck. Upper-level predators like barracuda and jacks are always the first to arrive on a new shipwreck, but they are swiftly followed by the spectrum of fish and invertebrates. As the wreck matures, and encrusting corals and sponges grow thick, it will support a burgeoning marine life population.

The project to sink *Spiegel Grove* in the waters off Key Largo was initiated in 1994 by a small group from the local business community, who enlisted the help and support of Monroe County, the Key Largo Chamber of Commerce, the state of Florida, the U.S. Navy, the U.S. Coast Guard, the U.S. Maritime Administration and the Florida Keys National Marine Sanctuary. The ship will be thoroughly cleaned and inspected prior to the sinking to avoid any possible contamination. The interior of the superstructure will also be opened and marked to allow safe diver access. Penetration below the prepared areas will be dangerous and is not recommended. Be prepared to face strong currents at this site.

Wreck Diving

Wreck diving can be safe and fascinating. Penetration of shipwrecks, however, is a skilled specialty and should not be attempted without proper training. Wrecks are often unstable; they can be silty, deep and disorienting. Use an experienced guide to view wrecks and the amazing coral communities that have developed on them.

17 *Benwood*

The old tale of a WWII German submarine torpedo attack still makes the rounds, but the true nature of this ship's sinking must have been only slightly less terrifying. British-built in 1910, the *Benwood* was 360ft long with a 51ft beam. Her last voyage began on April 6, 1942, when she left Tampa, Florida, for Norfolk, Virginia, loaded with phosphate rock.

Location: 3.5 nautical miles (6.7km) ESE of Mosquito Bank light

Depth Range: 25-45ft (8-14m)

Access: Boat

Expertise Rating: Novice

You'll find schoolmasters and porkfish amid the remains of this former bombing target.

The *Benwood* was running without navigation lights, as required at the time due to the possibility of attack by German submarines. The 544ft tanker *Robert C. Tuttle* was headed in the opposite direction, also without lights. Unfortunately, both vessels veered off course. In the blackness of 1 in the morning on April 9, the *Benwood's* bow smashed into the port side of the *Tuttle*. Desperate to save his ship, the *Benwood's* captain deliberately grounded the stricken vessel on the reef about six miles south of The Elbow. After

rescuing the crew of the *Benwood*, the *Tuttle* made it safely to port.

Over the years the wreck was used for bombing practice by the military and was intentionally demolished as a hazard to navigation. Now reduced to the crumpled but intact bow section, the bottom of the hull and scattered metal plating, the *Benwood* is one of the fishiest dives in a fishy sanctuary. Marked by four mooring buoys and one spar buoy, the wreck is about 25ft deep at her stern and 45ft at her bow.

The remaining structures and shallow depth make this an excellent choice for underwater photography, as well as a great night dive. The reds, yellows and purples of the encrusting sponges and corals come alive under the beam of your dive light. Macrophotographers will find hundreds of subjects at night on the wreck.

Benwood's **Outside Wall** is a deeper feature at about 80ft that few divers see because the wreck takes up all their bottom time. More like a terrace, this site is immediately seaward of the *Benwood* and is reached fairly easily from the outer mooring buoy. Chances are good of spotting a turtle or other large animal among the scattered corals here.

18 French Reef

French Reef is best known for its swim-throughs and caverns. As on other outer bank reefs, the coral ridges run in roughly parallel lines from shallow water to deep, though on French they twist and turn, transforming the reef into a living maze. The high-profile coral ridges evoke big city streets lined with tall buildings. In some places the ridges are fused into a single wide wall; in others just the tops are joined, forming elegant arches. Circular pockets with sand bottoms have formed in several areas, especially toward the north end of the reef. Depths on the main reef range from about 12 to 40ft. The water gets steadily deeper as you move seaward away from the coral ridges, but the most interesting part of the reef is fairly shallow.

Location: 2 nautical miles (3.8km) NE of Molasses Reef light

Depth Range: 12-40ft (4-12m)

Access: Boat

Expertise Rating: Intermediate

You may notice that live coral coverage is somewhat sparse compared to other reefs, but healthy colonies of elkhorn, star and brain corals are still scattered about the reef. Thanks to the reef's designation as a sanctuary preservation area, all common reef fish species are abundant, particularly parrotfish. Stoplight and queen parrotfish nibble

French Reef offers several swim-throughs, such as this undercut ridge dubbed Hourglass Cave.

the corals singly and in pairs, while midnight parrotfish scavenge in schools of a dozen or more.

French Reef encompasses many individual dive sites, including **Hourglass Cave**, named for its hourglass-shaped supporting pillar, and **Christmas Tree Cave**, which is topped with a somewhat tree-shaped star coral formation—provided your imagination is limber enough.

The latter is about 6ft wide, 4ft high and 15 to 20ft long. Two other caves at French are **Sand Bottom Cave**, which of course has a smooth white-sand floor, and **Hard Bottom Cave**, with a gray fossil coral floor. None of the arches or caverns at French Reef are difficult to traverse, but care should be taken not to injure marine life on the bottom or overhead as you pass through.

19 White Bank (North & South)

Visited almost exclusively by snorkel boats, this site is also called White Bank Coral Garden and White Bank Dry Rocks. The site includes two shallow reefs separated by a narrow channel. The reeftop is within a few feet of the surface in many spots, and the maximum depth is about 18ft. The northern section of White Bank is composed of one large, dense area of corals with several smaller adjacent patches, while the southern section is made up of smaller clusters. Reef grazers such as butterflyfish and parrotfish are plentiful here, as well as bicolor and yellowtail damselfish.

White Bank is more than a mile closer to shore than French Reef, affording it more protection from waves when the wind is up. The tradeoff is limited visi-

Location: 2 nautical miles (3.8km) north of Molasses Reef light

Depth Range: Surface-18ft (6m)

Access: Boat

Expertise Rating: Novice

bility. Green water and 20ft of visibility are about average for the site.

The reef here gets lots of abuse, as it is visited primarily by snorkelers trying the sport for the first time. Too many beginners over the years have gotten a mouthful of water, panicked and stood up on the coral, but White Bank continues to fascinate.

20 Three Sisters

This site was named for a trio of navigation aids that used to mark a shipping channel running from Molasses Reef to Hawk Channel. Large vessels don't pass that way anymore, but the day markers were left in place as reference points for boaters heading out to the reef line from Key Largo. Only two of the markers remain, and when they corrode beyond

Location: 3 nautical miles (5.7km) ESE of Rodriguez Key

Depth Range: 10-20ft (3-6m)

Access: Boat

Expertise Rating: Novice

maintaining, they too will be removed from the site.

Three Sisters is a series of shallow patch reefs. The largest is to the northwest of the site, while a string of smaller reefs trails off to the southeast. Depths range from 10ft on the flat dome of the reeftop to 18 or 20ft on the surrounding sand. The reefs to the southeast are close enough together that you can swim from one to the other if your navigation is up to the task.

While used frequently by fishermen, Three Sisters is overlooked by divers unless the weather kicks up. Regardless of the weather, it's a nice site to snorkel or just poke around on scuba. Macrophotography here is excellent, with numerous subjects just the right size for macro tubes or a close-up lens. Look for common invertebrates such as Christmas tree worms, arrow crabs, flamingo tongues and painted tunicates. If you're lucky and quick, you may be able to frame some colorful juvenile reef fish amid the coral heads, including queen, French and gray angelfish and spotted drums.

Christmas tree worms boast flower-like crowns.

21 | Sand Island

Less than 50 years ago Sand Island actually was an island. The natural forces of wave action and storm surge have removed the sand, leaving a very shallow carpet of coral rubble in the back reef. Amid several small spurs and scattered coral patches are two major coral fingers, neither as high as those on neighboring Molasses or French Reefs.

The depth at the middle of the three mooring buoys at Sand Island is about 14ft. Swimming seaward, you may discover a large bowl-like depression about 22ft deep, formed by the two main ridges. Hawksbill turtles and nurse sharks often

Location: .8 nautical miles (1.5km) NE of Molasses Reef light

Depth Range: 12-60ft (4-18m)

Access: Boat

Expertise Rating: Intermediate

rest on the sand here, and it's always a good place to stop for a while and let the reef "equalize" around you. Most of us spend far too much time moving quickly about the reef, and as a consequence, most of the fish we see are swimming away from us. Stop for even five minutes in the Florida Keys, and they'll come back to check you out. Stay in one place for 10 minutes and you'll be just another part of their world.

From the sand bowl the reef bottom slopes gently down to about 30ft. Scattered sea plumes and sea rods dominate this section of the reef, along with the occasional flattened head of star or brain coral. As at French Reef to the north, parrotfish are abundant at Sand Island. On this rather plain part of the site you'll likely encounter roving bands of blue parrotfish, munching their way along the reef. They're actually scraping the live polyps and algae from the coral, but they ingest pieces of the reef at the same time. The coral fragments are ground to fine sand in their gullets and excreted back onto the reef. An active parrotfish can churn out more than 2lbs of sand a day. Groups of six or seven, like the blue parrotfish patrols at Sand Island, can make up to a ton of sand each year.

22 Molasses Reef (North End)

Depths on this section of Molasses Reef range from 10 to 40ft, although a determined swim could bring you to much deeper water. The shallow end of the coral spurs are covered edge to edge with common sea fans and topped with small colonies of elkhorn coral. Pieces of an old tower are scattered across many of the sand channels.

The deeper end of the coral spurs are buttressed by exceptionally large star coral mounds. If you use a half inch per year as the growth rate, these heads are three or four centuries old. Some of them show the ravages of time, undercut by erosion and invaded by boring sponges; others have an even coat of tiny brown or green polyps and are still going strong.

Location: 4.5 nautical miles (8.6km) SE of Rodriguez Key

Depth Range: 10-40ft (3-12m)

Access: Boat

Expertise Rating: Intermediate

The real magic of Molasses Reef is the fish life. Bring along a waterproof fish ID book and you could easily mark off two dozen species on a single dive—many more if you're familiar with Florida reef fish. Even snorkeling at the surface, you'll be face to face with sergeant majors, Bermuda chub, barracuda and yellowtail snappers. In the mid-range, from 20 to 30ft, Molasses is a mob of reef fish.

The MV *Wellwood* ran aground on the north end of Molasses Reef in August 1984, grinding the coral beneath it into parking lot smoothness. The ship's owners incurred a settlement of more than $5 million, money that now primarily supports reef restoration efforts.

You'll see hordes of Bermuda chub and creole wrasses.

Massive star coral mounds at Molasses Reef are several centuries old and bear the scars to prove it.

23 Molasses Reef (Deep)

Three mooring buoys mark the deep reef at Molasses, a distinctly different part of the reef. Depths at the buoys range from 45 to 55ft, and the bottom consists of low coral ridges and narrow sand channels. Corals are plentiful, but are lower profile than on the shallower sections of the reef, except for the lush soft corals that grow to their tallest here. At this depth the sponges begin to dominate, particularly giant barrel sponges and elephant ear sponges. Bring a dive

Location: 4.5 nautical miles (8.6km) SE of Rodriguez Key

Depth Range: 40-90ft (12-27m)

Access: Boat

Expertise Rating: Advanced

light to appreciate their range of color. Queen angelfish, rock beauties and whitespotted filefish are permanent residents, and hawksbill turtles, spotted eagle rays and nurse sharks are frequently encountered.

If you follow the sand channels seaward, they will guide you down a gentle slope until you reach a lip at 65 or 70ft. At this point a mini-wall drops to about 90ft, joining a relatively flat sand bottom with widely scattered coral heads. The edge of the wall is a highway of sorts for large pelagic fish, so it's worth spending a little time here if your profile permits.

When a current is present, it can be strong enough to challenge even advanced divers, so take note before you enter the water. Several Key Largo shops make drift dives on the deep section at Molasses, precluding any navigation problems and opening up even more of the reef to exploration.

Whitespotted filefish feed in pairs on gorgonians and sponges.

24 Molasses Reef (South End)

Location: 4.5 nautical miles (8.6km) SE of Rodriguez Key

Depth Range: 10-40ft (3-12m)

Access: Boat

Expertise Rating: Intermediate

When a current is running at Molasses Reef, it's usually strongest at the south end. The reef looks much different when being swept by currents, and not only because the soft corals bend with the flow. The myriad grunts, snappers and wrasses that normally fill the mid-water instead hug the sides of the coral ridges in the lee of the reef. There is a curiously empty appearance to the reef, until you realize where all the fish have gone.

The southernmost buoy marks **Permit Ledge**, a long coral-and-sponge-covered ledge facing sand flats and a low hard bottom. Divers here often encounter large animals, including permits, spotted eagle rays and nurse sharks. Cross the flats south of Permit Ledge and you'll come to another ledge, this one topped with five or six colonies of pillar coral.

Slightly to the north is a site called **Fire Coral Caves**, where a deeply undercut coral ledge harbors Atlantic spadefish, dog snappers and schoolmasters. A large jewfish sometimes hovers beneath the ledge, and half a dozen permits frequently hang about the area. Some fire coral grows atop the ridge, but the reddish hue in the caves is due to the encrusting corals and sponges.

The **Spanish Anchor** is a bit northeast of Fire Coral Caves, lying flat on the bottom. Farther to the north is the **Winch Hole**, where a large coral-encrusted windlass is all that remains of a ship that ran aground on Molasses long ago. Along the coral ridge, **Hole in the Wall** is a split that leads into an oval chamber.

A dog snapper rests at Fire Coral Caves, where walls are painted in encrusting sponges and corals.

25 *Bibb*

Built for the U.S. Coast Guard in 1936, the *Bibb* is a 327ft cutter with a 41ft beam. One of the Secretary class, this ship was named for former U.S. Secretary of the Treasury George M. Bibb. She was powered by twin Westinghouse steam turbines and had the range to go anywhere in the world.

Location: 1 nautical mile (1.9km) south of Molasses Reef light

Depth Range: 95-130ft (29-40m)

Access: Boat

Expertise Rating: Advanced

During the first part of WWII the *Bibb* escorted convoys in the North Atlantic, Caribbean and Mediterranean. In 1943 the *Bibb*'s crew saved 202 people when the troopship SS *Henry Mallory* was torpedoed by the German submarine U-*402*. That same night the *Bibb* also rescued 33 sailors from the torpedoed freighter SS *Kalliopi*. When the European theater began to draw to a close, she was reassigned to the Pacific, taking part in the battle for Okinawa in 1945. The *Bibb* also served in Vietnam in 1968 and '69.

A group of local businesses and dive shops formed the Key Largo Artificial Reef Association and worked with the National Marine Sanctuary to sink the *Bibb* south of Molasses Reef in 1987. The ship initially went down without a problem, but she listed during the sinking and landed on her starboard side in 130ft. Corals and sponges thickly encrust the masts, superstructure and propeller. Since the superstructure lies parallel to the bottom in relatively deep water, the predators and reef fish on the *Bibb* are not as visible as they might have been had the ship settled upright. Expect to meet a few patrolling barracuda on the way down the buoy line, though. They are merely the advance guard for a dense population of resident fish and invertebrates.

Penetration of the wreck can be very hazardous due to the depth and sideways orientation of the vessel and should only be made by divers with the proper training, equipment and experience. The shallowest point of the wreck is the port deck rail, about 95ft deep. The sand bottom is about

The *Bibb*'s anchor windlass is a kaleidoscope of living color.

130ft deep. Visibility is normally 40 to 100ft. Currents can be very strong and vary quickly. Be prepared to show evidence of recent deep dives or advanced certification prior to diving the *Bibb* with a local dive shop.

26 *Duane*

Also built in 1936, and named in honor of former U.S. Secretary of the Treasury William J. Duane, this 327ft Coast Guard cutter is a sister ship of the cutter *Bibb*. The two ships are only about a quarter mile apart on the bottom, not far from Molasses Reef. As far back as 1940 the *Duane* and the *Bibb* worked together, coordinating their efforts as weather stations in the North Atlantic.

Location: 1.2 nautical miles (2.3km) south of Molasses Reef light

Depth Range: 50-115ft (15-35m)

Access: Boat

Expertise Rating: Advanced

While serving as a convoy escort in 1942, the *Duane* assisted in rescuing 229 people when the troop-carrying passenger ship SS *Dorchester* was torpedoed by the German submarine U-*233*. In a joint attack with her sister ship the *Spencer* the following year, the *Duane* forced the submarine U-*175* to the surface with depth charges and took 22 of its crew prisoner as the sub sank. At Normandy the *Duane* was the flagship of Maj. Gen. John O'Daniel, head of Operation Dragoon during the invasion of France.

The *Duane* patrolled the coast of Vietnam between 1957 and 1968 as part of the Coastal Surveillance Force. In 1980 the cutter actually steamed over the spot where she now rests, on the way to Key West for escort duty during the massive Mariel Boatlift, which brought nearly 125,000 Cuban refugees to the Florida Keys. During her 50-year career, however, the *Duane*'s most important accomplishment is the number of lives saved during rescue operations.

The *Duane* sits upright on the sand, with a maximum depth of 115ft. The superstructure is accessible down to the main deck, and the interior of the bridge is laced with yellow rope sponge. The ship's masts reach to within 50ft of the surface, attracting a squadron of very large great barracuda. Schools of crevalle jacks and permits patrol the wreck, and the hull is home to a huge variety of fish, including many angelfish and parrotfish.

As on the *Bibb*, currents can develop quickly and be very strong. Evidence of advanced diving experience may be required before a dive shop will take you to either wreck.

27　Pickles

Common sea fans cover the crest of Pickles so thickly it looks like a sea fan farm. The 19th century wreck that gives this reef its name also lies in the shallows, in about 10ft of water near two metal stakes that mark the reeftop. The Pickle Barrel Wreck was a barge that carried mortar in wooden barrels, possibly for the construction of Fort Jefferson in the Dry Tortugas. The wood of the barrels is long gone, but seawater set up the mortar, and a number of barrel-shaped concrete plugs litter the bottom. The sides of the vessel are surprisingly intact for such an exposed wreck and shelter many juvenile fish and invertebrates.

Location: 4 nautical miles (7.6km) SE of Rodriguez Key

Depth Range: 10-80ft (3-24m)

Access: Boat

Expertise Rating: Intermediate

Three mooring buoys are in place at Pickles. Depth at the buoys is about 15ft. A short snorkel toward land will take you along the reef crest; if you head seaward on scuba, you'll descend a gradual slope to 70 or 80ft before the reef peters out.

The highlights of the reef, though, are near the buoys. Several wedge-shaped sand channels run past the buoys. The sides are formed by 5ft-high coral ledges that are undercut 2 to 3ft. During the day hundreds of grunts and snappers line the ledges, giving way graciously to the parrotfish that munch their way along the coral. Several large, healthy colonies of star, starlet and brain corals sit in isolation on the sand.

When you first enter the water, look carefully around at the limits of your vision. Turtles and nurse sharks often shelter along the margins of the sand channels and can be closely approached if you are patient and careful.

Mortar plugs retain their "pickle barrel" shape.

Plantation & Upper Matecumbe Keys

Once you cross the bridge over Tavernier Creek, you'll find more dive shops, restaurants and a small marina. Plantation Yacht Harbor Resort (MM 87) has a sandy beach with watersports equipment rentals in addition to the marina and restaurant. Nearby are two places to shop for gifts and local crafts: the Rain Barrel Artists Village and Treasure Village. South of the drawbridge over Snake Creek, Windley Key offers the Theater of the Sea theme park (MM 84.5) and Holiday Isle (MM 84), a center for deep-sea fishing, backcountry fishing, watersports and general partying.

Esteemed by fishers as spirited game fish, the tarpon at Robbie's opt for easy pickings.

More sportfishing and backcountry boats are based south of the Whale Harbor Channel bridge.

Between Upper and Lower Matecumbe is Indian Key, on the ocean side of the highway, which was the southern boundary of Dade County until 1866. On the bay side is Lignumvitae Key, a historic and botanical site accessible by boat.

Dive shops and other facilities are less concentrated between Upper Matecumbe and Marathon, reflecting the gap between dive sites. Dozens of huge silver tarpon gather off the docks at Robbie's (MM 77.5), waiting to be hand-fed buckets of baitfish. Long Key State Park (MM 67.5) offers a beach, fishing, camping and canoe trails.

Plantation & Upper Matecumbe Keys

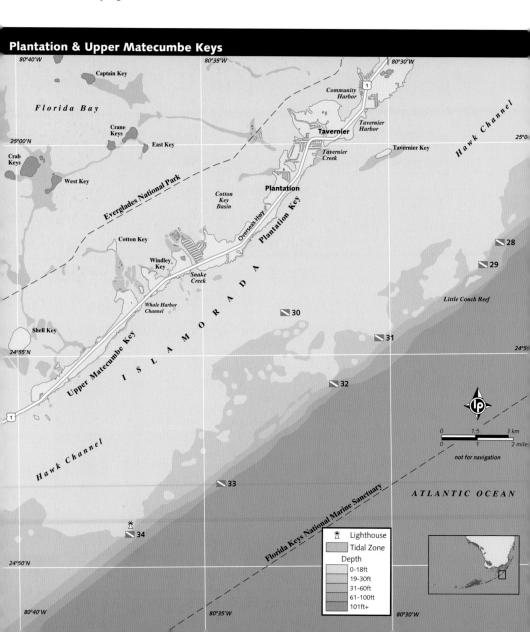

Plantation & Upper Matecumbe Keys Dive Sites

	Good Snorkeling	Novice	Intermediate	Advanced
28 Conch Wall				●
29 Conch Reef	●		●	
30 Hen & Chickens	●	●		
31 Davis Reef	●	●		
32 Crocker Reef			●	
33 *Eagle*				●
34 Alligator Reef	●		●	

28 | Conch Wall

One of the few places in the Florida Keys where the reef forms anything resembling a vertical wall, Conch Wall is a nice change of pace. Dropping steeply from 60 to 90ft, this is one of the deepest living reefs in the Florida Keys. The wall is festooned with deepwater sea fans and several species of barrel sponges, including giant, leathery and green barrel sponges. You'll see lots of red and purple finger sponges, too.

Angelfish, parrotfish, wrasses and other reef fish are plentiful along the wall, but it's the possibility of seeing larger animals that cranks the excitement of diving here up a notch. Big jacks, like the speedy crevalle jacks, are nearly always around. Greater amberjacks and permits show up from time to time, while you'll likely spot several species of grouper, including black, Nassau and yellowfin groupers.

Drift dive Conch Wall when a current is running—which is most of the time—and you'll feel like you're flying. Choosing your entry point and timing your descent can be tricky, but then you can relax and

Location: 3.5 nautical miles (6.7km) SE of Tavernier Key

Depth Range: 60-90ft (18-27m)

Access: Boat

Expertise Rating: Advanced

go with the flow. Toward the end of your dive, you can either ascend directly to a safety stop or head up a prominent sand chute to shallower water atop Conch Reef.

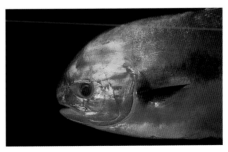

Permits may approach to give you a once-over.

29 Conch Reef

The once ubiquitous queen conch are regaining their former numbers at sites throughout the Keys, but don't expect to see any while you're scuba diving on Conch Reef. Put on a snorkel and check out the sand flats and seagrass behind the reef crest, though, and you'll see quite a lot of them grazing in the grass.

Conch Reef is the current home of the Aquarius undersea research center. Free public access would interrupt many of the research projects underway at Aquarius, so the area around the underwater lab is marked off with yellow buoys and

Location: 3.5 nautical miles (6.7km) SE of Tavernier Key

Depth Range: 18-60ft (6-18m)

Access: Boat

Expertise Rating: Intermediate

restricted to those with sanctuary research permits. Resist the temptation to see what's going on, otherwise you may find the sanctuary patrol waiting when you return to your boat.

Anyway, the reef outside the research zone has plenty to offer. Conch Reef is slightly deeper than neighboring reefs, so it's thick with gorgonians and barrel sponges, lending the topography a lush fullness. Look beyond the waving sea plumes and sea rods, though, and you'll also find many medium-sized star and boulder brain corals. Snappers and hogfish are particularly plentiful on Conch Reef. Hog snappers like to cruise among the gorgonians as they feed, and schoolmasters gather in small schools near the ledges.

Hawksbill turtles frequent the reef, perhaps because sponges, a primary source of food for this species, are abundant here. Early morning, late afternoon and night are the most likely times to

Queen conchs are mounting a comeback from overharvesting. encounter them.

Research on the Reef

Originally constructed in the mid-1980s for the National Oceanic and Atmospheric Administration's (NOAA) National Undersea Research Program, the Aquarius underwater laboratory was first deployed off St. Croix in the U.S. Virgin Islands. In 1993 the system was moved to the Florida Keys, after being refurbished by the University of North Carolina at Wilmington (UNCW), which operates the lab in partnership with NOAA.

The Aquarius lab consists of three main components: the habitat itself, an 81-ton double-lock decompression chamber that measures 12ft in diameter by 43ft long; the baseplate, a 116-ton steel structure that supports the habitat; and the mission control center, which is 9 miles away on Key Largo and is linked to the habitat by wireless telemetry.

The principal benefit of the habitat is increased bottom time provided by saturation diving. Scientists live in the habitat for missions lasting up to 14 days, avoiding the need to return to the surface after a short dive or to decompress after a long dive. At the end of the mission, the pressure in the habitat is gradually reduced over a 17-hour period, decompressing the researchers as they rest or continue to work.

More than 50 missions have been completed since Aquarius was deployed in the Florida Keys, investigating water quality, coral biology, fisheries assessments and global climate change. The laboratory is in about 60ft (18m) of water at Conch Reef. Access to the site is restricted to research permit holders only, but anyone can visit the lab website at www.uncwil.edu/nurc/aquarius.

30 Hen & Chickens

Marked by a light tower, Hen & Chickens is a popular spot for three reasons. The first is its convenient location, less than 2 nautical miles from shore, almost in the middle of Hawk Channel. The second is that it's protected from rough seas. When high winds bring waves to the outer reefs, Hen & Chickens experiences a comfortable chop; when the seas are calm, Hen & Chickens is like a swimming pool with a living bottom. The

Location: 2 nautical miles (3.8km) ESE of Snake Creek

Depth Range: 5-20ft (2-6m)

Access: Boat

Expertise Rating: Novice

third reason is that the reef structure itself is fascinating.

The site comprises a series of enormous mounds of hard-coral colonies, principally star and brain corals. These are mature colonies, several hundred years old, that have built up their imposing structures bit by tiny bit. Once the hard corals were established, soft corals, sponges and algae found places to settle in, creating the mixed habitat you see today. Expect to see a wide variety of grazing fish at Hen & Chickens, including stoplight parrotfish, gray angelfish and surgeonfish. These and other related species pick at the algae, corals and sponges.

The downside of Hen & Chickens' nearshore position is limited visibility. Generally the reef is bathed in green water,

The sun-dappled shallows support a wide mix of marine life.

and any surge tends to stir up sediments from the bottom. Expect to encounter moderate currents during peak tidal flow. Twenty to 30ft of visibility is a worthwhile trade-off, though, when the weather keeps you off the main reefs, and of course there are numerous days when even Hen & Chickens sparkles in clear water, especially during the summer months.

31 Davis Reef

A 2ft bronze statue of a seated Buddha was placed in the sand at the south end of Davis Reef in 1989. Buddha's head and belly are highly polished from the hands of all the divers who've rubbed the statue for good luck. An even smaller standing Buddha appears to be propping up a magnificent globe of smooth brain coral about 20ft away.

Location: 4 nautical miles (7.6km) south of Tavernier Key

Depth Range: 15-30ft (5-9m)

Access: Boat

Expertise Rating: Novice

The topography at Davis Reef is very different from other nearby reefs. Four mooring buoys are in place on the main part of the reef, a long coral ledge running generally north-south. Landward of the ledge is a long sand flat, speckled with softball-sized hard corals and diminutive sea plumes. The ledge is the central attraction at Davis, rising 4 or 5ft above the sand and undercut deeply in places. Orange elephant ear sponges encrust the underside and face of the ledge, and hundreds of Caesar grunts, schoolmasters and bluestriped grunts shelter cheek to cheek alongside the ledge.

If you cross perpendicular to the ledge and swim seaward, you'll pass over a fairly uniform hard bottom with some scattered hard corals, including one very large and healthy starlet coral toward the north end of the reef. Most of these isolated coral mounds are cleaning stations, where juvenile Spanish hogfish and neon gobies eat the ectoparasites off bar jacks and other customers. After 150 to 200ft the hard bottom peters out, giving way to a vast sandy plain covered with large sea plumes and dozens of black loggerhead sponges.

Buddha's hand-polished belly beckons divers.

32 | Crocker Reef

Marked by red nun buoy No. 16, Crocker is not a sanctuary preservation area, so expect heavy fishing boat traffic, especially on the weekends. Two moorings are in place, one in about 55ft and one in 40ft. Starting a dive from the shallower buoy, you'll find low-profile coral fingers topped with large star coral heads, as well as a few convoluted and smooth brain corals. Giant barrel, leathery barrel and brown tube sponges grow in large numbers on the fingers, along with many sea fans and sea plumes. The fingers are not continuous, but run toward deeper water in a broken pattern, gradually becoming more dense.

Location: 4 nautical miles (7.6km) SE of Snake Creek

Depth Range: 17-90ft (5-27m)

Access: Boat

Expertise Rating: Intermediate

The sand channels are generally quite narrow, though in some places the reef fingers open up, creating spacious sand pockets. A sizeable population of yellowhead jawfish lives in the pockets, hovering vertically over their holes as they pluck bits of

Jawfish hover vertically.

food from the water. Blue angelfish are also common on this section of Crocker Reef, as are rock beauties and honeycomb cowfish.

A long swim seaward will take you down a very gentle slope until you finally reach the shelf break at 60ft. The reef drops away steeply here, then levels out on a sandy plain at about 90ft. Currents often sweep the site, especially along the shelf break. This is an active zone, with big schools of bluestriped grunts, schoolmasters and creole wrasses hugging the coral on top.

The hard-bottom reef crest at Crocker is about 17ft deep, supporting scattered plate-sized heads of hard coral and many soft corals. Blue tangs, yellowtail snappers and a variety of damselfish are among the reef fish common in this shallow area.

33 | *Eagle*

This 269ft freighter sailed with the names *Raila Dan*, *Barok*, *Carmela*, *Ytai*, *Etai*, *Carigulf Pioneer* and *Aaron K* painted on her stern before she became the MV *Eagle* in acknowledgement of the Eagle Tire Co.'s financial support in the effort to sink her as an artificial reef.

Launched in Holland in 1962, she was capable of cruising at 12.5 knots,

Location: 5 nautical miles (9.5km) south of Snake Creek

Depth Range: 70-120ft (21-37m)

Access: Boat

Expertise Rating: Advanced

powered by a 10-cylinder diesel engine. Under the name *Aaron K* the ship transported newspaper and cardboard from the U.S. to Central and South America. A serious fire broke out while the ship was en route from Miami to Venezuela in 1985, damaging much of the electrical system and machinery of the vessel beyond repair.

Declared a total loss by the insurers, the ship was towed to Miami. Members of the Islamorada diving community, looking for a suitable ship to sink, found her there and made the arrangements to have the ship cleaned and towed to the Keys. On December 19, 1985, high explosives were used to blow holes in the hull, sinking the freighter in less than two minutes.

Unfortunately, *Eagle* settled on her starboard side, giving the ship a deeper profile than intended and exposing some of the jagged metal from the blasts. The ship is a great deep dive, though, with lots of coral-encrusted rigging, including the crow's nest and two masts. Depth to the port rail is about 70ft, and the bottom is between 110 and 120ft.

In 1998 the powerful storm surge of Hurricane Georges broke the hull in two, leaving a V-shaped gap amidships and opening sections of the interior that were previously inaccessible. Because of the depth, sideways orientation and storm damage, penetration of the wreck should be attempted only by trained divers with proper equipment. Guided penetrations are available from several local shops.

Strong currents are common on the wreck, supporting the entire food chain. In addition to thousands of reef fish, expect to see predators like great barracuda and crevalle jacks. Big, silvery tarpon are also permanent residents.

Divers approach the crow's nest on the *Eagle*, which lies on her starboard side in 120ft (37m).

34 Alligator Reef

This reef was named for the ship that was lost here in 1822. The USS *Alligator*, an 86ft, 12-cannon schooner, was constructed in Boston for the U.S. Navy to combat slavery and piracy. After a few initial successes, the ship unfortunately ran aground on this reef and was blown up by the crew to keep it from falling into the hands of pirates.

Location: 5 nautical miles (9.5km) south of Whale Harbor Channel

Depth Range: 10-50ft (3-15m)

Access: Boat

Expertise Rating: Intermediate

A lighthouse was scheduled to be built on Alligator Reef in 1857, but was put off until after the Civil War. The existing lighthouse was finally completed in 1873. The buoy closest to the lighthouse marks the spot where ballast stones and other bits of the *Alligator* wreckage lie in about 10ft of water. The four buoys southeast of the lighthouse are aligned along the edge of the main reef.

The coral ridges at Alligator are somewhat flattened, forming an extensive system of low but deeply undercut ledges lined with encrusting sponges and corals. These ledges support a variety of invertebrates, including arrow crabs, spiny lobsters and Spanish lobsters. Caesar and French grunts are abundant, schooling atop the ledges or sheltering in their lee when a current is running. Depths here range from about 20ft on the back reef to 50ft on the seaward side.

Seeing the Light

When you dive on one of the Florida Keys reefs marked by a lighthouse, take a moment to look up at the light. Better yet, snorkel over to examine the unique way it's fastened directly to the reef. Built about 150 years ago, these remarkable lighthouses are no longer manned, but they still guide vessels away from the reefs with automatic lights. The original design of the lights called for massive brick foundations, which would have been an ecological disaster for the reefs. The screw-pile design that was adopted minimizes contact with the reef and allows water to circulate freely beneath the structure.

Middle Keys Dive Sites

The large passes to the east and west of the Middle Keys allow more mixing of Florida Bay and Atlantic Ocean waters, reducing the concentration of coral reefs. There are still many nice places to dive—they're just spread over a greater area. Ashore, the Dolphin Research Center on Grassy Key (MM 59) provides educational and entertaining dolphin encounters. For beachgoers, Curry Hammock State Park (MM 56) offers a shallow-water beach, picnic tables, barbecue pits and restrooms, while Sombrero Beach (MM 50) has a deepwater beach, playground, picnic grounds and restrooms.

Marathon, a former fishing port and construction camp now second only to Key West in size, is a rather metropolitan part of the Keys, with a hospital and headquarters for the Florida Highway Patrol, Florida Marine Patrol and Florida Keys National Marine Sanctuary. Naturally, it is the focal point for this region's dive shops, with dive boats based in Key Colony Beach, Marathon Shores and the Faro Blanco Marine Resort.

The Marathon Airport (MM 52) offers limited connections to Miami and other Florida cities. Sightseeing and seaplane rides are available, and this airport is home

This stretch of sand at Curry Hammock State Park is among the handful of beaches in the Keys.

base for the fleet of DC-3s that spray the Keys for mosquitoes. Just east of the Seven Mile Bridge, Boot Key Harbor is one of the largest and most protected anchorages in the Keys.

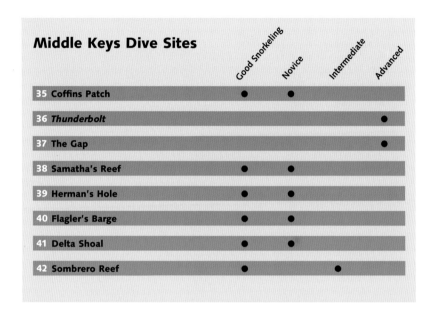

Middle Keys Dive Sites	Good Snorkeling	Novice	Intermediate	Advanced
35 Coffins Patch	●	●		
36 *Thunderbolt*				●
37 The Gap				●
38 Samatha's Reef	●	●		
39 Herman's Hole	●	●		
40 Flagler's Barge	●	●		
41 Delta Shoal	●	●		
42 Sombrero Reef	●		●	

Middle Keys

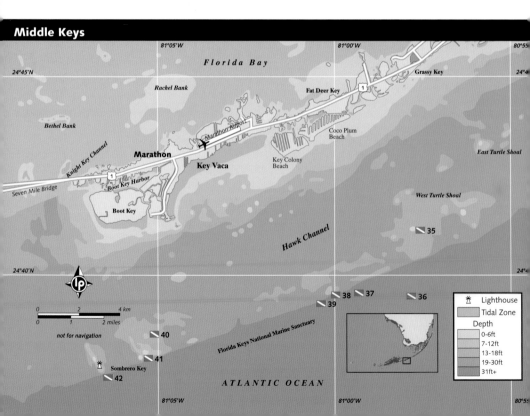

35 Coffins Patch

This reef was labeled Coffin's Patches on early marine charts, suggesting it may have been named after a person, though stories circulate of a ship that ran aground here while carrying a load of coffins. The reef is on the long sand bank that runs seaward of Hawk Channel. Depths range from 15 to 25ft, with flat, irregularly shaped mounds of coral enclosing scattered sand pockets.

Location: 4 nautical miles (7.6km) SE of Key Colony Beach

Depth Range: 15-25ft (5-8m)

Access: Boat

Expertise Rating: Novice

Southern stingrays often rest or feed atop the sand at Coffins Patch. If you hang back a few minutes to acclimate the ray to your presence, it may let you approach very closely. Rays feed primarily on mollusks and other invertebrates that are buried in the sand. They locate their prey with finely tuned senses similar to a shark's, then suck the hapless victims out of the sand, using their blunt jaws with fused teeth to crush the shells. Watch one feed and you'll see the sand being vented out through their gill slits.

The west end of the reef features extensive pillar coral formations. Most hard corals rely on the symbiotic algae within their tissues for energy during the day and keep their polyps retracted until nighttime. But pillar coral polyps feed actively in daylight, and their extended tentacles give this coral a fuzzy appearance. Its daytime feeding habit and slender skeletal pillars make this coral very susceptible to damage from divers.

As on most of the inshore reefs, visibility is highly variable at Coffins Patch. Most of the time it will be around 30ft, but it can be as high as 50 or 60ft or as low as 10 or 15ft. If you arrive when visibility is down, don't fret. The reef is always packed with life—just narrow your focus and enjoy the show.

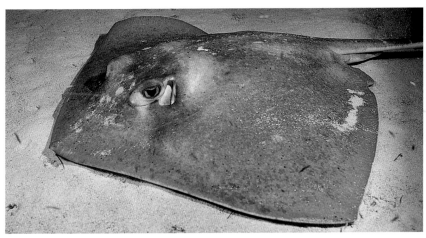

Often lying motionless atop or concealed beneath sand, southern stingrays are easily approached.

36 *Thunderbolt*

This 188ft vessel was built in 1942 for the U.S. Army. Originally designed as a cable layer, she still has the huge open-spoked cable wheel mounted on the forward deck. *Thunderbolt*'s real thrills, though, came after she was retired by the military and purchased by Florida Power & Light for research into lightning strikes. A turbine engine was mounted on the aft deck to churn out lightning-attracting ions as the ship plowed through storms.

The ship was set to begin another career, this time in underwater surveying, when she sank while docked on the Miami River. The dive operators and businesses in Marathon collected money

Location: 5 nautical miles (9.5km) SE of Key Colony Beach

Depth Range: 75-120ft (23-37m)

Access: Boat

Expertise Rating: Advanced

to have *Thunderbolt* cleaned and towed to the Keys, where she was quietly scuttled on March 3, 1986.

The top of the superstructure is about 75ft deep, and the cable wheel is at about 85ft. The entire wheelhouse and lower crew's quarters are accessible. The first divers down will nearly always find a couple of barracuda guarding the bridge. As you work your way aft, you'll swim through swirling clouds of jacks and grunts. The sponges and algae that coat the wreck attract many grazers, including French and queen angelfish, rock beauties and several species of parrotfish.

The engine compartments are wide open, allowing easy entry into the deepest part of the ship. The aft deck and the sides of the hull are liberally covered with gorgonians and small mounds of hard coral. The depth on the bottom next to the exposed twin screws is about 120ft. If you look carefully, welded letters on the ship's stern reveal her original name to be USS *Randolph*.

Watch out for fire coral on the subsurface float and the line going down to the ship. Gloves aren't recommended in most of the national marine sanctuary, but strong currents are common here, and you may need gloves to protect your hands during the descent and ascent.

The cable wheel attracts cruising barracuda.

37 The Gap

Two nautical miles southwest of Coffins Patch, The Gap is a wide cut on the edge of the shelf. The depth atop the cut is about 50ft. From the reeftop, the bottom slopes steeply downward, terminating in a flat sand bottom 75 to 80ft deep. You may encounter strong currents at this site, especially in this deep section. The coral cover is thickest close to the edge of the drop-off, thinning into isolated patches on the sand.

Several species of reef fish frequently congregate in schools and loose packs along the top of the gap, including bar jacks, schoolmasters and creole wrasses. French angelfish and rock beauties are nearly always present, staying close to the coral along the slope and nibbling on the sponges. Green barrel sponges and

Location: 4 nautical miles (7.6km) SSE of Key Colony Beach

Depth Range: 50-80ft (15-24m)

Access: Boat

Expertise Rating: Advanced

deepwater sea fans stand among the sea plumes and giant star corals scattered along the slope face.

The boundary between the bottom of the slope and the sand flats is a corridor of sorts for pelagic animals. It's worth investing a few minutes of your bottom time here, in case any jacks, rays or sharks come cruising past.

French angelfish are common along the reef slope and allow divers to approach rather closely.

38 Samatha's Reef

Long, winding ledges with deeply under-cut sides are the defining characteristic of Samatha's Reef. The depth is about 14ft atop the ledges and 25ft at the large oval sand patch in the middle of the reef. Heading south, you'll gradually reach water 30 to 35ft deep, but your best bet is to move east and west, following the ledges. Medium-sized colonies of smooth and grooved brain corals and smooth globes of starlet coral are scattered along the upper surfaces of the ledges, along with an assortment of soft corals and tube sponges. Cracks bisect the ledges, opening narrow gaps that shelter numerous squirrelfish and blackbar soldierfish.

The fish are very active at Samatha's, streaming constantly along the ledges like commuters going to work. Small-mouth grunts, surgeonfish and yellowtail snappers gather in mixed groups, then parade off to their next stop on the reef. Schools of gray Bermuda chub are also

Location: 3.5 nautical miles (6.7km) south of Key Colony Beach

Depth Range: 14-35ft (4-11m)

Access: Boat

Expertise Rating: Novice

abundant here, swimming more aggressively above the coral.

The nurse sharks at Samatha's are unfazed by divers, having been fed by local dive operators for years. In fact, if you stop in a sand pocket, they may swim boldly up to you. Enjoy the encounter or make the most of the photo op, but keep your hands and fingers tucked away so they aren't mistaken for bait. A number of exceptionally large and equally pushy southern stingrays are also drawn here by the feeding activity.

Usually shy and lethargic, the nurse sharks at Samatha's are used to being fed—and often.

To Feed or Not to Feed?

While fish feeding is not currently prohibited by sanctuary regulations or state law, it is highly discouraged. Sure, if you throw a crust of bread on the water, you'll bring a swarm of Bermuda chub and sergeant majors to the surface, but you don't have to do that to see fish up close in the Florida Keys. You'll see hundreds of fish schooling, reproducing and feeding naturally on every dive.

Novice divers and snorkelers think it's fun to feed the fish, but they soon discover they've only created a nuisance. When the food runs out, the fish may nip at your hair and fingers. Worse still, if you feed the fish around your boat, that's where they'll stay. While you dive or snorkel the reef, many of the fish will linger around your boat or the next one, waiting for handouts.

Is fish feeding dangerous? In the Florida Keys two potentially dangerous species are sometimes hand-fed: green morays and great barracuda. Yes, it's thrilling to see them up close and watch them eat, but both of these fish can inflict a serious wound in the blink of an eye. Let the professionals feed and handle these animals. When you're diving on sites where these fish are fed, especially during an actual feeding, keep your hands by your sides and your fingers folded against your palms. Waggling fingertips look temptingly like bait to a hungry barracuda or eel.

Fish feeding modifies normal fish behavior and alters their natural diet. Both of these changes are detrimental to the health of the fish population. If you must succumb to the temptation to feed the fish anyway, please do not give them bread, cheese or other human food. Some dive shops offer specially prepared fish food tablets or sticks. At least these will provide the right nutrients.

Captain Slate has been mouth-to-mouth feeding the barracuda at the *City of Washington* for years.

39 Herman's Hole

A large, sandy hole marks the center of Herman's Hole. Depths here range from 15 to 30ft, and the reeftop features a nice balance of hard corals, gorgonians and sponges. Some of the common sea fans are huge, and there are several unblemished spheres of smooth brain coral. Branching vase sponges are abundant, and you'll see lots of orange encrusting

Location: 3.5 nautical miles (6.7km) south of Key Colony Beach

Depth Range: 15-30ft (5-9m)

Access: Boat

Expertise Rating: Novice

sponges if you peer down into the cracks that split the reeftop occasionally.

Think small to spot curious roughhead blennies.

Two species of rays often rest or feed in the circular sand pockets—large gray southern stingrays and smaller, yellow-and-black yellow stingrays. Nurse sharks sometimes rest on the sand, too, usually around the margin of the pocket or in the many smaller sand channels on the reef.

A long ledge forms the northern edge of the reef, its face undercut and split by numerous small ravines. Everyone sees the squirrelfish, bluestriped grunts and porkfish that gather here, but too many divers hurry along the ledge like it's a highway with a minimum speed limit. The diversity of marine life that finds shelter here is amazing. Cut your throttles back to idle and you'll find fascinating animals like bold little roughhead blennies, vividly colored juvenile queen angelfish and corkscrew anemones with their symbiotic Pederson cleaner shrimp.

40 Flagler's Barge

This shallow wreck is also called the Delta Shoal Barge or simply The Barge. Although the exact origin of the vessel is unknown, it probably carried construction materials and supplies to Marathon during repair work on Flagler's Overseas Railroad in the 1920s or '30s. One hundred feet long and 30ft wide, it sits in 20ft of water on a flat sand bottom. Both ends slope upward, a design that allowed it to be towed in either direction. Much of the side plating has corroded away, leaving an exposed framework of steel I-beams that support the remaining deck and hull sections. The entire wreck is easily accessible to divers.

Over time the sea has transformed the barge into an incredibly effective artificial reef. The interior is liberally coated with white telesto corals and a colorful assort-

Location: 1.6 nautical miles (3km) NE of Sombrero Key

Depth Range: 10-20ft (3-6m)

Access: Boat

Expertise Rating: Novice

ment of encrusting sponges. Sea fans, plumes and rods carpet every available surface at each end of the wreck.

Fish life is equally impressive. Macro and close-up photographers could spend a week here and still not see everything the site has to offer. High-hats, normally difficult to find and photograph, swim freely in large numbers. Mixed schools of bluestriped, French and Caesar grunts, mangrove snappers, schoolmasters and yellowtail goatfish crowd each of the interior compartments. Caribbean giant anemones adorn the hull and crossbeams in several places.

If you tire of fish-watching on the barge, take a swing around the surrounding terrain. Nurse sharks and rays often rest on the sand, and the turtle grass beds boast an ecology all their own.

Soft corals and sponges coat every inch of Flagler's Barge, attracting dozens of marine species.

41 Delta Shoal

The remains of a navigation tower lie scattered over the shallowest portion of Delta Shoal, in about 7ft of water. In the same area, a slave ship known as the Ivory Coast Wreck ran aground in 1853. Only a determined search will locate any sign of the old ship now, but numerous artifacts were recovered here in the past.

Like most Florida reefs, Delta Shoal consists of a series of coral-covered ridges, aligned perpendicular to the distant shore. Schooling tomtates and French grunts are particularly numerous along the sides and on top of the fingers. Rock beauties and queen angelfish are

Location: 1 nautical mile (1.9km) ENE of Sombrero Key

Depth Range: 7-25ft (2-8m)

Access: Boat

Expertise Rating: Novice

also abundant, placidly munching on clustered brown tube and orange elephant ear sponges. The maximum depth at the seaward end of the ridges is just below 25ft.

It's possible to tour the entire reef on one dive, but you'd miss much of the scenery. A better way to see a shallow reef like this is to stay in one place. Anchor yourself next to a coral ridge with one fin tip resting gently in the sand, cross your arms and relax. Stay as motionless as possible, breathing lightly and evenly. You may feel foolish, but within a few minutes the fish will grow accustomed to your presence, stop perceiving you as a possible threat, and the reef will come alive.

Elephant ear sponges grow up to 6ft (2m) wide.

42 Sombrero Reef

Named by early Spanish explorers, Sombrero Reef is opposite the east end of the Seven Mile Bridge. The reef is marked by the 142ft Sombrero Key Light, which was built in 1858, before the key itself eroded away. The light was automated in 1960.

As at most outer bank reefs in the Keys, the main feature of Sombrero Reef is an extensive spur-and-groove system. Long, parallel coral-topped ridges are aligned laterally across the reef, separated by low sand channels. The depth at the shallow end is about 6ft to the top of the spurs and 10ft to the bottom. Maximum depth along the ends of the spurs is about 30ft.

Most of the living coral cover is atop the spurs, where exposure to currents and

Location: 3.5 nautical miles (6.7km) south of Boot Key

Depth Range: 6-75ft (2-23m)

Access: Boat

Expertise Rating: Intermediate

sunlight is greatest, though competition for space relegates some colonies to the sides, as well as on the exposed hard bottom in the sand channels. A wide variety of encrusting sponges, which are not dependent on sunlight, coat the sides and undercut surfaces of the ridges. At a feature known as "The Arch," the undercut ridge forms a graceful span.

Fish often attach their eggs to the spur walls for protection until they hatch. The purple smear of sergeant major egg masses are common in this part of the reef, guarded by frantic males while other fish try to sneak a free meal. Anemones are also common in the crevices alongside the ridges, with only their tentacles exposed to view.

Giant anemones reach out from reef crevices.

Lower Keys & Key West Dive Sites

Of the 42 bridges in the Florida Keys, none is more familiar than the Seven Mile Bridge, a backdrop in numerous advertisements and movies. Starting at MM 47, the bridge spans Moser Channel, stretching from the west end of Vaca Key to Little Duck Key. Most of the Old Seven Mile Bridge still stands, providing a nice pier for fishermen and access to the national historic district on Pigeon Key. Once a work camp, Pigeon Key later served as a research station and now features a museum, picnic grounds and snorkeling.

The main access to Looe (pronounced loo) Key and the surrounding reefs and wrecks is from dive shops between Bahia Honda and Cudjoe Key. Bahia Honda State Park (MM 37) offers camping and several gorgeous beaches—one of the few public stretches between Marathon and Key West.

Lower Keys & Key West Dive Sites	Good Snorkeling	Novice	Intermediate	Advanced
43 Newfound Harbor	●	●		
44 Looe Key (East End)	●		●	
45 Looe Key (West End)	●		●	
46 Looe Key (Deep)			●	
47 *Adolphus Busch Sr.*				●
48 Western Sambo	●	●		
49 Joe's Tug			●	
50 Toppino's Buoy	●	●		
51 9-Foot Stake	●	●		
52 *Cayman Salvage Master*				●
53 Eastern Dry Rocks	●	●		
54 Rock Key	●	●		
55 Sand Key Reef	●		●	
56 Western Dry Rocks	●	●		
57 Marquesas Keys	●		●	

Big Pine and No Name Keys are the sole habitat of the endangered Key deer, a diminutive relative of the Virginia whitetail. A full-grown adult is less than 3ft (1m) high at the shoulder and weighs about 60lbs (27kg). Only about 300 of these tiny creatures remain. Most Key deer fatalities are from collisions with cars, so the reduced speed limit in the National Key Deer Refuge and surrounding area is taken very seriously. Feeding the deer is also illegal.

As you pass Cudjoe Key, look to the north for a glimpse of "Fat Albert," a tethered blimp used for electronic surveillance of the airspace between the Keys and Cuba. Perky's Bat Tower on Sugarloaf Key (MM 17) was the brainchild of resort owner R.C. Perky, who built the tower in 1929 and stocked it with bats imported from Texas to eat mosquitoes. Unfortunately, once he released the bats, they departed for good. The Saddlebunch Keys are a scattered group of low mangrove islands preceding Boca Chica Key, home of the Key West Naval Air Station. Next in line is Stock Island, which takes its name from the herds of cattle and pigs once kept there. The island is home to Oceanside Marina, one of several full-service marinas in the Key West area.

Historic Key West is the principal tourist destination and largest port in the Keys. In addition to its marinas and many dive shops, the town is chock-full of tourist attractions. After you've had your fill of the maritime museums, the aquarium, the gift shops and superb art galleries, there is still the Hemingway House, Ripley's Believe It or Not! and the buoy at the southernmost point in the continental U.S., at the corner of South and Whitehead Streets. Key West beaches include

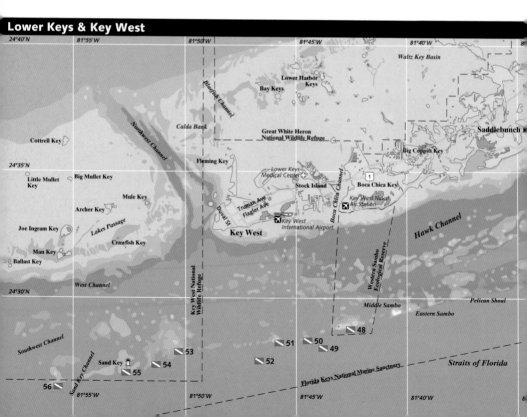

Lower Keys & Key West

Smathers Beach on South Roosevelt Boulevard, Clarence Higgs Memorial Beach on Atlantic Boulevard and South Beach at the end of Duval Street. Set aside time for at least one sunset at Mallory Square, where the end of the day sparks a colorful celebration.

As the islands of the Florida Keys curve to the west, the reefs are sheltered from winds out of the north and northeast, often blessing the dive sites in this region with good conditions. All Lower Keys dive sites are within the Florida Keys National Marine Sanctuary.

Rotating acts hog the spotlight in Key West's Mallory Square.

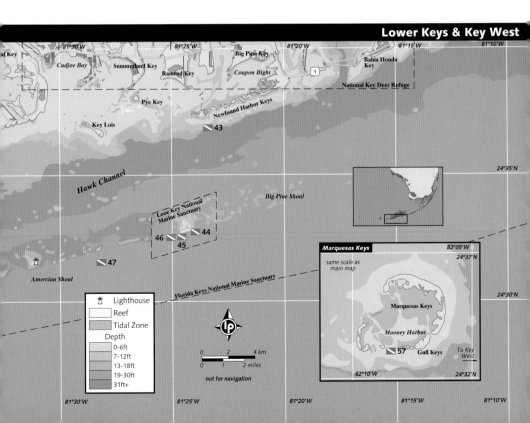

Lower Keys & Key West

43 Newfound Harbor

Closer to shore than most other reefs, this sanctuary preservation area is a good choice for snorkeling or as an alternative when weather prevents diving at nearby Looe Key. Just northwest is low-lying Little Palm Island, now home to an exclusive resort. The namesake palm trees were planted in the '60s to lend the island a South Pacific look when it was used as the setting for the movie *PT-109*.

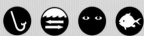

Location: .5 nautical miles (1km) south of Newfound Harbor Keys

Depth Range: Surface-15ft (5m)

Access: Boat

Expertise Rating: Novice

A series of mooring buoys are in place along the west side of the reef, and day marker No. 50 lies to the south. The top of the reef is very shallow, rising almost to the surface in two places. Maximum depth is about 8ft on the landward side and 15ft on the seaward side. Soft corals dominate much of the reef, but boulder-like accumulations of calcium carbonate from hard corals form the basic structure.

Fishermen frequented the reef until the summer of 1997 when the SPA went into effect, and the resident fish population has been steadily increasing ever since. Snappers and grunts in particular

have benefited from the additional protection. Gray snappers and Caesar grunts are found here in large numbers, along with occasional mutton snappers and French grunts. Like most inshore reefs, Newfound Harbor is also a nursery ground for the outer reefs, and juveniles of many reef fish are present.

Nearshore currents give the water a greenish cast and limit visibility to about 20ft, though visibility improves during incoming tides and periods of low wind. When the winds are up, reduced visibility is a reasonable trade-off for this site's calm dive conditions.

44 Looe Key (East End)

Looe Key takes its name from the wreck of HMS *Looe*, a 46-gun frigate built in 1741. Commanded by Capt. Ashby Utting, the warship was sent to protect British interests along the Florida and Georgia coastline. In 1744 the *Looe* captured a suspected Spanish vessel sailing under a French flag and took the ship under tow. But early in the morning on February 5, the *Looe* ran aground on the east end of the reef. Remnants of the ship remain at about 25ft, though don't expect to find them without a knowledgeable guide.

Location: 4.5 nautical miles (8.6km) south of Newfound Harbor Keys

Depth Range: 10-35ft (3-11m)

Access: Boat

Expertise Rating: Intermediate

The reef consists of parallel limestone ridges, built up over the past five or six millennia from the excreted calcium carbonate of coral polyps. Living coral flourishes atop these ridges and on isolated coral heads in the sand channels between them. The depth is about 10ft near the reef crest, sloping to 35ft at the end of the ridges.

Although hard corals such as star and brain corals thrive here, there is also a healthy concentration of soft corals. Common sea fans grow at all depths, while sea plumes, sea rods and sea whips are plentiful below 15ft. Many soft corals look so much like trees, it's easy to forget they are colonial animals like hard corals. Soft corals, though, have flexible skeletons and polyps with eight tentacles, instead of the six tentacles of hard corals.

Naturally, this is also a good spot to find inverte-brates that feed on gorgonians, like distinctively patterned flamingo tongues or the spiky bristle worm. Look for these creatures near the base of the colony or along one of the arms.

Flamingo tongues mate on a gorgonian branch.

45 Looe Key (West End)

At the heart of the Looe Key National Marine Sanctuary, the west end of this classic outer bank reef supports a greater buildup of boulder corals than the east end. A high-profile spur-and-groove formation begins in 10 to 12ft of water, sloping to 35ft at the seaward end. Huge colonies of brain, star and giant star corals grow one on top of the other—national treasures on a par with California's great redwoods. Many of these masters of reef building have been alive for more than three centuries.

Toward the reef crest the ridges are narrow and close together, the channel between them only 2 or 3ft wide in some places. Deep undercuts are common,

Location: 4.5 nautical miles (8.6km) south of Newfound Harbor Keys

Depth Range: Surface-35ft (11m)

Access: Boat

Expertise Rating: Intermediate

usually lined with rows of clustered brown tube or orange elephant ear sponges. Branching corals, principally elkhorn with a few smaller colonies of antler, grow in the shallows, thriving in the surge that flows over the ridges. As you swim seaward, the ridges flatten and spread out.

The shallow, rubble-capped reef crest gives way to an expansive back reef of sand flats and thick seagrass beds. Even snorkelers must exercise caution near the reef crest, where depths can be less than a foot.

Fishing and lobstering have been prohibited here for 20 years, and the fish have grown accustomed to divers. As you swim through aggregations of yellowtail snappers, sergeant majors, surgeonfish and French grunts, they will barely expend the energy to get out of your way. Larger fish, like barracuda, mutton snappers and Nassau groupers, will eyeball you cautiously but hold their ground.

Anything but the Theme from *Jaws*

The Florida Keys National Marine Sanctuary and the Lower Keys Chamber of Commerce (☎ 800-872-3722; www.lowerkeyschamber.com) stage the annual Lower Keys Underwater Music Festival each July at Looe Key. US1 Radio (104.1 FM) broadcasts a selection of music, ranging from rock to country, classical and blues, which is piped into the water via underwater speakers on participating dive boats. Dive to your favorite tunes and see what music the fish like best. Now, if they can just figure out how to take live requests.

46 Looe Key (Deep)

Below the dramatic coral ridges of the Looe Key fore reef, the terrain gives way to a gently sloping plain, ending in the sand at about 80ft. At first glance it may look dull, but what you're seeing is a fertile transition zone—from big corals to big sponges and from high-profile ridges to low furrows and narrow sand channels.

This is the deep reef, where you're more likely to see fast-swimming jacks, angelfish and pairs of filefish than the mixed schools of grunts, damselfish and snappers one finds on the fore reef. The hard corals are still present—they're just low-profile at this depth. Sea plumes and sea rods grow taller here than in the shallows, and beginning around 50ft you'll find colonies of deepwater sea fans.

Sponges are plentiful, including many giant barrel sponges. It's difficult to swim past their tall chimneys without taking a peek inside. Most are empty, as the inside is the excurrent opening—the output vent of the sponge's digestive system.

Location: 4.5 nautical miles (8.6km) south of Newfound Harbor Keys

Depth Range: 40-80ft (12-24m)

Access: Boat

Expertise Rating: Intermediate

Occasionally, though, you'll find something surprising, like a green moray, a channel clinging crab or even a colony of *Porites* coral. In late summer the sponges reproduce en masse, expelling smoky clouds of eggs or sperm.

Navigation is easy on the deep reef, as the parallel ridges and sand channels are still present, though less prominent than on the fore reef. Following the channels will take you to either deeper or shallower water, and crossing the ridges will take you laterally across the reef. Strong currents are common at this site.

Current-swept slopes on the deep reef at Looe Key support deepwater sea fans and sponges.

Where Do Baby Corals Come From?

The mass spawning of corals in the Florida Keys is a fascinating phenomenon. Five to eight nights after the first full moon in August, corals simultaneously release billions of gametes. They float to the surface like an upside-down underwater snowstorm, drifting away to begin the cycle of life from larvae to polyps. The branching corals, like elkhorn and staghorn, tend to spawn at the beginning of this period, followed by the boulder corals like star and giant star.

A number of dive operators run special trips for divers who wish to witness the event. The spawning usually occurs fairly late at night, often between 11pm and midnight, so the trip is part dive, part social event and part science as divers wait for the rush to begin. Witnessing this unique event is worth the effort.

47 *Adolphus Busch Sr.*

Built in Scotland in 1951, this 210ft coastal freighter sailed the Atlantic, Great Lakes and Caribbean under the names *London*, *Windsor Trader*, *Topsail Star* and *Ocean Alley* before the Looe Key Artificial Reef Association found her languishing at the dock in Port-au-Prince, Haiti. With the generous support of Adolphus Busch IV, the association purchased the vessel and towed it to Miami for an extensive cleanup and preparations to make it diver safe. Oil, fuel and other possible contaminants were removed, along with hatches and doors that might impede diver egress.

The ship, renamed *Adolphus Busch Sr.* after the patriarch of the brewing family, was carefully anchored a few miles west of Looe Key on December 5, 1998, and gently scuttled in 105ft of water. She landed upright on the sandy bottom, secured in position by two bow anchors and one stern anchor. Because of the depth and frequent strong currents, local dive shops may require proof of advanced certification and recently logged deep dives.

Four mooring buoys are arrayed along the starboard side of the ship, whose bow points south. The shallowest

Location: 3.5 nautical miles (6.7km) west of Looe Key

Depth Range: 50-105ft (15-32m)

Access: Boat

Expertise Rating: Advanced

spot on the wreck is a small mast on the wheelhouse, about 50ft deep, just beside a shorter radar antenna tower. It's about 65ft to the top of the wheelhouse itself. Another mast and the anchor windlass add some vertical dimension to the foredeck, while the main deck is at 85ft. You can swim right down into the open holds and explore the tiered decks around their perimeter.

Colorful encrusting sponges and corals are slowly taking hold, improving the *Busch*'s effectiveness as an artificial reef. The ship was an immediate draw for fish life, though, attracting a pair of large jewfish soon after she hit the bottom. Reef fish swarm all over the wreck, especially around the wheelhouse, where thousands of Caesar grunts have taken

A diver enters the wheelhouse of the *Busch* as a gray angelfish looks on from the window.

up residence. Several great barracuda also roam the wreck, carefully checking out each group of visiting divers.

After diving the wreck, go out and rent a copy of *Fire Down Below*, the 1957 film starring Robert Mitchum, Jack Lemmon and Rita Hayworth, to see the *Busch* in her previous life. The disaster staged on the ship for the movie seems a haunting premonition of things to come.

48 | Western Sambo

This extensive reef south of Boca Chica has been designated an ecological reserve, a special protected zone similar to a sanctuary preservation area. Unlike an SPA, however, which safeguards frequently visited reefs, an ER is a larger site intended to provide sheltered spawning and nursery grounds for marine life in the sanctuary. The reserve's rectangular dimensions extend from the shoreline to beyond the outer reef, encompassing mangrove, seagrass, hard bottom, sand bottom and coral reef habitats. In the years since the ER was implemented, divers have noticed significant increases in both vertebrate and invertebrate populations.

Mooring buoys mark more than a dozen dive sites east to west along the

Location: 4.5 nautical miles (8.6km) south of Boca Chica Key

Depth Range: 15-45ft (5-14m)

Access: Boat

Expertise Rating: Novice

reef, with depths ranging from about 20 to 35ft. Three of the most popular sites are Cannonball Cut, Haystacks and The Lounge.

Cannonball Cut features a distinctive channel between coral spurs on the east end of the reef, with an unusually large population of spiny lobsters. **Haystacks**

takes its name from the size and shape of the large star coral colonies that have been growing here for several centuries. Overshadowed by the massive star corals are a number of smooth brain corals that have also witnessed the passage of many decades. Buoy No. 8 marks **The Lounge**, an open area adjacent to a cut through the coral. A boat rudder from a past grounding incident still lies on the bottom.

Colonies of mountainous star coral take on the shape of haystacks at Western Sambo.

49 Joe's Tug

Stripped of its engine and propeller and filled with scraps of steel, Joe's Tug was destined for duty as an artificial reef off Miami. The details of how it sank prematurely in 60ft of water south of Key West on January 21, 1989, have been lost over the years. The story may differ with every telling now, but that's part of this little ship's appeal.

Location: 5.5 nautical miles (10km) south of Stock Island

Depth Range: 50-60ft (15-18m)

Access: Boat

Expertise Rating: Intermediate

The wreck is a steel harbor tug about 75ft long, built with a small wheelhouse well forward and a clear afterdeck. Intact for many years, its large rudder eventually fell to the bottom after the rudder post gave way. In 1998 Hurricane Georges tore off the wheelhouse, depositing most of it upside down off the port side. A year later Hurricane Irene cracked the hull amidships, but the tug still sits upright with only a slight list to port. Be prepared to face a moderate current.

Although it's a small wreck, it supports a wealth of marine life. Schoolmasters are always present in large numbers, along with many French and bluestriped grunts. A pair of green morays usually come out to greet divers, and an old loggerhead turtle is often in residence.

Joe's Tug is a delightful night dive if you're looking for something different than a shallow reef. Under cover of darkness the hull is decorated with basket stars, and spiny lobsters wander the decks in search of food.

A foray on the surrounding reef is also worthwhile. In addition to soft sea plumes and colonies of giant star coral, you'll find exquisite leathery barrel sponges. Named for their tough, smooth brown texture, these sponges host a wide range of invertebrates within their tissues. Light one up with your dive light to bring out the brighter red and orange of encrusting organisms.

Leave the tug to find leathery barrel sponges.

50 Toppino's Buoy

This shallow site is also known as Marker 1, which was formerly the number of the navigation marker here, or Marker 32, the current marker number. The site is composed of seven or eight coral fingers, oriented north-south. Depths are about

Location: 5 nautical miles (9.5km) south of Stock Island

Depth Range: 12-30ft (4-9m)

Access: Boat

Expertise Rating: Novice

12ft atop the fingers and 22ft in the sand. From the seaward end of the fingers a hard bottom slopes into deeper water, though it's a long swim by the time you reach 30ft. The flats are sprinkled with moderate-sized hard and soft corals, but most of the action is between the fingers.

Hundreds of fish hang about the coral walls, not separated by species. Margates, scrawled filefish, banded butterflyfish, bluestriped grunts, surgeonfish, smallmouth grunts and gray snappers all mingle together, weaving a colorful tapestry. You might see a pair of spotfin butterflyfish pecking at one

Foureye butterflyfish often school in pairs.

coral head and a pair of foureye butter-flys right next door. The ledges also attract larger animals, like nurse sharks and hawksbill turtles. Green turtles are also frequent visitors.

Near the west end of the reef you'll find an unusual arching colony of pillar coral. Growing on what appears to be the rim of an ancient brain coral, the pillars cover an arc about 6ft long. Corals are somewhat sparse atop the fingers, but sea plumes and sea fans sprout from the sides, and starlet coral formations are scattered in the sand.

Toppino's is a popular night dive, as it's shallow and marked by a navigation light. Divers easily find their way along the reef, which is equally lively at night.

51 9-Foot Stake

Don't expect to find this site's namesake stake—a wooden pole that supported a navigation marker atop the shallowest part of the reef (9ft at low tide). A passing boat dislodged it several years ago.

The sprawling, shallow reef features long, winding ledges that connect moder-ate-sized mounds of coral. One of the big surprises here is a massive head of smooth brain coral. So old that most of its foun-dation has eroded, the colony sits atop one of the coral patches, surrounded by

Location: 5 nautical miles (9.5km) south of Key West

Depth Range: 9-20ft (3-6m)

Access: Boat

Expertise Rating: Novice

bluestriped and French grunts. The max-imum depth at 9-Foot Stake is about 20ft.

Fascinating macro life includes the otherworldy arrow crab, with a lance-like rostrum, or snout.

Spiny lobsters, spotted morays, stoplight parrotfish and foureye butterflyfish are common here, but many divers flock here to photograph its smaller residents. Macrophotographers in particular will love this reef. Take any 10 sq ft section and you'll find lots of juvenile reef fish and marine invertebrates for subjects. At night the selection gets even better.

While you're in macro mode, check out the range of creatures that make themselves at home on a sponge here. Sponges are often covered in parasitic zooanthids, a close cousin to the sea anemone. Arrow crabs, brittle stars, coral shrimp and a variety of hydroids are among the hundreds of other species that find shelter within a sponge.

52 *Cayman Salvage Master*

Built in 1937 by Pusey & Jones shipyard in Wilmington, Delaware, as a minelayer for the U.S. Army Mine Planter Service, the *Cayman Salvage Master* was originally named the *Lt. Col. Ellery W. Niles.* Before ending up on the bottom off Key West, she played several other roles, including service as a cable layer in the Army Signal Corps, a research vessel

Location: 5.5 nautical miles (10km) south of Key West

Depth Range: 65-90ft (20-27m)

Access: Boat

Expertise Rating: Advanced

The storied ship's large cable spool provides a focal point for fish and divers alike.

for TRACOR of Miami, a freighter under Panamanian registry and, in her final incarnation, a salvage vessel under Cayman Islands registry.

In 1980 the ship was confiscated by the government for illegally carrying Cuban refugees during the Mariel Boatlift. The next three years were spent tied to the dock in Key West, until the ship sank in place from neglect. After she was refloated, her pilothouse was removed, and the vessel was slated to be sunk in deep water, primarily as a fish magnet for sportfishing. On the way to the designated site in April 1985, the *Cayman Salvage Master* again sank prematurely, landing on her port side in 90ft of water. Later that same year the storm surge from Hurricane Kate rolled the ship upright.

The *Cayman Salvage Master* is 187ft long with a 37ft beam. Minus its superstructure, the wreck still rises 26ft from the bottom. As the starboard hull rested face up for the first half year after the ship sank, that side in particular is covered with swaying soft corals. The spoked cable spool still graces the bow and is a focal point on the wreck, always surrounded by schools of grunts, jacks and damselfish.

Although some openings breach the hull, the *Cayman Salvage Master* is not a good wreck for penetration. Thick cables and other obstacles block the entrances, and there is very little maneuvering room inside. Strong currents are common. A trio of bicycles was recently left on the main deck, offering some additional entertainment to the dive.

53 Eastern Dry Rocks

This is a favorite spot for snorkel boats out of Key West. The combination of high visitation and strong surge has reduced the live coral cover over the years, but much of the reef is still healthy, and there are lots of fish.

The reef crest at Eastern Dry Rocks is nearly three-quarters of a mile long, oriented generally east-west. Most of the mooring buoys are along the west end of the reef, which is generally the leeward side. One additional buoy is on the back reef.

New elkhorn coral recruits have sprouted up in several places, particularly in the shallows along the southern edge. These new colonies grow upward at a 45° angle in branches less than a foot long. Take care not to kick them, as they'll break easily, destroying two or three years' worth of growth.

Location: 2 nautical miles (3.8km) ENE of Sand Key

Depth Range: Surface-30ft (9m)

Access: Boat

Expertise Rating: Novice

To the north the reef gives way to flats of finely ground coral rubble, sand and seagrass. A variety of invertebrates and juvenile fish live in this zone, and a wide range of herbivores depend on it for food. To the south the reef slopes quickly down to 30ft, then eases down to 70 or 75ft. Most of the coral is concentrated in the top 30ft, though more soft corals and sponges reside in the lower half.

54 Rock Key

A diamond-shaped day marker warns of shallow water on this reef midway between Sand Key and Eastern Dry Rocks, and the reeftop is even exposed at low tide. The best diving is between 10 and 30ft, along a prominent sand channel that runs through the middle of the reef. Ridges on the west side form a canyon with deeply undercut sides. The undersides of the ledges are painted bright yellow and orange by encrusting sponges, though the colors only come alive when lit by a strobe or powerful dive light. Below 30ft the live coral cover is sparse, and the bottom is flat.

Rock Key is one of 18 sanctuary preservation areas in the Keys. The prohibition against all means of marine life harvesting, including hook-and-line fishing, has dramatically increased the fish pop-

Location: 1 nautical mile (1.9km) east of Sand Key

Depth Range: Surface-30ft (9m)

Access: Boat

Expertise Rating: Novice

ulation. Yellowtail snappers, bluestriped grunts and sergeant majors are among the most abundant, but all of the common species are present.

This site presents a good alternative when all the buoys are occupied at Sand Key. It's also a nice spot when you don't want to spend the whole dive swimming like crazy. You can take it easy here and still see most of the reef.

The Conch Republic

KEY WEST

Conchs are people who were born and raised in Key West. It's a difficult title to earn; even after seven years of living here you only rise to the rank of Freshwater Conch. You will no doubt hear (and see the flag) of the Conch Republic, and therein lies an interesting tale.

In 1982 the U.S. Border Patrol set up sporadic roadblocks on U.S. 1 just south of Florida City in an attempt to stop drug smugglers and illegal aliens driving up from the Keys. As traffic jams and anger mounted, many tourists decided to forgo the Keys altogether.

Enter a bunch of outraged Conchs, led by Key West Mayor Dennis Wardlow, who came up with the brilliant idea of seceding from the U.S. They established the nation of the Conch Republic on April 23, 1982, seceded from the U.S., rebelled for one minute, then surrendered and requested $1 billion in foreign aid and war relief.

Every April, Conchs celebrate the anniversary of those heady days.

55 Sand Key Reef

Sand Key is one of Key West's most popular snorkel spots. The shallow reef, sand island and towering lighthouse make it a wonderful place to spend a morning or afternoon taking in the sights above and below water. The exposed sand island is actually pulverized coral and shells. It does not support any vegetation and has shifted considerably in size, shape and location over the years.

Location: 6.5 nautical miles (12km) SW of Key West

Depth Range: 5-35ft (2-11m)

Access: Boat

Expertise Rating: Intermediate

The reef is extensive, with the parallel coral fingers and alternating sand channels typical of outer Florida Keys reefs. Only a few feet deep at the shallowest sections, Sand Key is great for snorkelers who just want to float on the surface and enjoy the show below. The deep end of the coral fingers is in about 35ft of water.

Move slowly to approach the myriad reef fish that feed on suspended plankton. Sergeant majors often feed in large schools near the surface, along with dozens of yellowtail snappers, creole wrasses and brown chromis. Closer to the reef, several species of damselfish defend their territory, and slender trumpetfish skulk among the coral branches in hopes of ambushing smaller fish.

Visibility is highly variable at Sand Key, due to strong surge and tidal flow. If you happen to visit when the water is cloudy, don't count it out. Next time the conditions may be splendid.

Trumpetfish change color and position to blend into the reef.

56 | Western Dry Rocks

This reef is suitable for both diving and snorkeling. The shallowest corals extend much farther north than on other reefs, with many interesting nooks for snorkelers to explore. The corals are so shallow that you can simply float at the surface to enjoy the marine life below. Golden brown branches of elkhorn coral grow atop many ridges.

Location: 3 nautical miles (5.7km) west of Sand Key

Depth Range: Surface-40ft (12m)

Access: Boat

Expertise Rating: Novice

You'll find lots of life amid the sponge- and coral-coated ledges, including shade-loving squirrelfish.

You may notice dead elkhorn branches, gray in color with a light film of algae. While it is one of the fastest-growing corals, elkhorn is also one of the shortest lived, though even dead colonies provide habitat and food for many fish. The tiny bicolor damselfish, for instance, zealously guards its "crop" of algae growth on the branches. These pugnacious little fish will even dart out and nip at a diver who lingers too long in their territory.

More accomplished snorkelers and divers can follow the many fractured ledges that wind through the reef in 10 to 15ft of water. Naturally, the sponges, corals and algae that grow on the sides of the ledges attract many fish, but life is everywhere in the Keys, even in the plain-looking sand. Nearly transparent goldspot and bridled gobies rest atop the sand or fine coral rubble on any reef, while shrimp, crabs, blennies and other fish often linger where the sand meets the reef.

Head south from the reef crest to reach deeper water. The gradual slope features a fairly smooth hard bottom sprinkled with medium-sized mounds of starlet and brain corals and a variety of gorgonians. Below 30ft you'll find more sponges, especially smaller giant barrel sponges. Going deeper than 35 or 40ft requires a lengthy swim away from the moorings atop the reef.

57 Marquesas Keys

Several dive and snorkel boats make the trip from Key West out to this atoll, typically offering a whole-day adventure with lunch on the beach. The water is shallow, mostly 10 to 20ft and sometimes even less, but there are many interesting wrecks and scattered reefs.

Currents can be strong during peak tidal flow, especially in the narrow cuts. Those same currents carry an abundance of food to sessile filter feeders, however, making the atoll a great place to find invertebrates like feather duster worms, Christmas tree worms and sea anemones. As the islands sit between the Gulf of Mexico and Straits of Florida, you'll likely encounter species from both areas.

The Spanish treasure galleon *Nuestra Señora de Atocha* foundered off the Marquesas in 1622 and was located by Mel

Location: 16 nautical miles (30km) west of Key West

Depth Range: Surface-20ft (6m)

Access: Boat or live-aboard

Expertise Rating: Intermediate

Fisher in 1985. Artifacts from the wreck, including gold bars, coins, weapons and delicate jewelry, are on display at his museum in Key West.

The military used the islands as a bombing and strafing range for many years, but the entire group is now protected within the Key West National Wildlife Refuge. Other than one or two privately owned houses, the islands are undeveloped.

Dry Tortugas Dive Sites

In the early 1800s the islands of the Dry Tortugas were considered vital to controlling U.S. interests in the Gulf of Mexico, though their strategic importance has been superceded by history. Fifty-five nautical miles (105km) beyond Key West, the archipelago's seven islands are protected within both Dry Tortugas National Park and the Florida Keys National Marine Sanctuary.

Ponce de León gave the name *Las Tortugas* (The Turtles) to these remote islands due to the large number of resident turtles. More pragmatic sailors noted the lack of fresh water and added "Dry" to the name. Preferring the scrubby vegetation, thousands of sooty and noddy terns congregate on Bush Key each spring to lay their eggs.

The National Park Service maintains a staff at historic Fort Jefferson and provides campsites on the beach outside the fort, but visitors to the Dry Tortugas must still be self-sufficient. Access to the islands is by ferry, seaplane, live-aboard or private boat. You can tie up to the dock in front of the fort for a few hours, but for longer stays you must move out slightly to the Garden Key anchorage.

Getting to the Tortugas

Following is a list of public transportation options to Dry Tortugas National Park. For information on services, contact the park at 305-242-7700 or visit the website at www.nps.gov/drto.

Dry Tortugas Ferry
Yankee Freedom II
☎ 305-294-7009
toll-free ☎ 800-634-0939
www.yankeefleet.com

Sunny Days Catamarans
Fast Cat II
☎ 305-292-6100
toll-free ☎ 800-236-7937
www.drytortugas.com
cattours@aol.com

Seaplanes of Key West
Key West International Airport
☎ 305-294-0709
toll-free ☎ 800-950-2359
www.seaplanesofkeywest.com
seaplanes@floridakeys.com

Fort Jefferson is a fascinating place to visit. Only partially completed at the start of the Civil War, it remained in Union hands. Sixteen million bricks went into the construction of the fort, and you can still see the difference between the original red bricks, which came from Southern states, and the orange bricks from the North. The fort never realized any strategic importance, but was used as a prison, counting Lincoln assassination conspirator Dr. Samuel Mudd among its inmates.

Diving and snorkeling opportunities in the Dry Tortugas are markedly different than in the rest of the Keys. Day visitors can snorkel around the fort on Garden Key, but you'll need a boat to reach other shallow sites like Windjammer and Loggerhead Reef. Much of the diving is on deep, pristine reefs, but their remoteness limits access to private boats, charters and live-aboards.

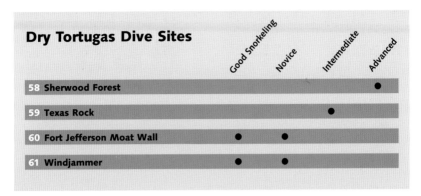

Dry Tortugas Dive Sites	Good Snorkeling	Novice	Intermediate	Advanced
58 Sherwood Forest				●
59 Texas Rock			●	
60 Fort Jefferson Moat Wall	●	●		
61 Windjammer	●	●		

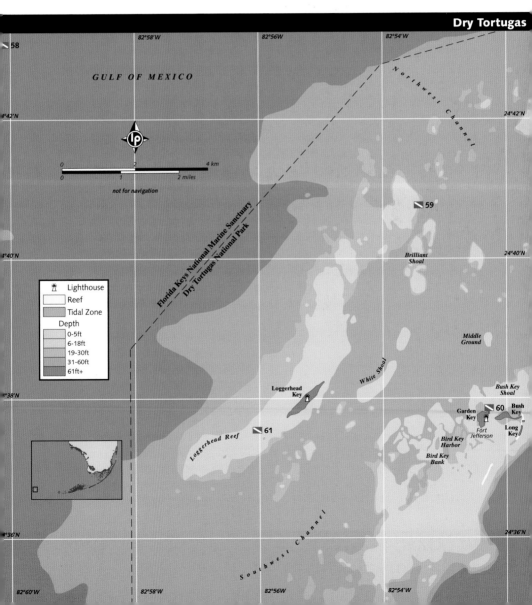

58 Sherwood Forest

In a section of the Dry Tortugas recently added to the Florida Keys National Marine Sanctuary, Sherwood Forest is a deep reef with a coral canopy, or "false bottom." The main reef structure is essentially a shelf about 80ft deep supported by a fossil coral foundation. Below the cracks and hollows you can see the sand bottom another 20ft below.

Location: 7 nautical miles (13km) NW of Loggerhead Key

Depth Range: 80-100ft (24-30m)

Access: Boat or live-aboard

Expertise Rating: Advanced

Colonies of star and giant star corals atop the shelf often grow in tall mushroom shapes to take advantage of the ambient sunlight and prevailing currents. Some of the giant star corals exhibit an unusual fluorescent pigmentation that tints them pinkish red. Several species of black coral also thrive here, often tucked into a small depression or clinging to the side of the shelf. Take extra care not to touch these colonies, as they are very susceptible to damage.

You'll find the Keys' usual variety of angelfish, snapper, grunts, surgeonfish, damselfish and parrotfish, but you may see a few surprises in the water column above the coral. Fast-swimming predators like cero and Spanish mackerel often pass by, sometimes swerving for a closer look at divers.

The location and depth of Sherwood Forest usually ensure exceptionally clear, blue water. Currents are sometimes strong at this site.

59 Texas Rock

Almost due north of Garden Key in Dry Tortugas National Park, Texas Rock looks more like a site you'd find in Jamaica or parts of Grand Cayman than the Florida Keys. The predictable spur-and-groove formation and gradual slope from shallow to deep is replaced by random peaks and valleys. The sand bottom is about 50ft deep, but much of the reef is less than 18ft deep. The reef face is nearly vertical in most places, and often deeply undercut, creating overhangs 10 and 20ft wide. Unblemished colonies of star and giant star coral grow on top of these meandering ledges, while the underside sprouts a thick beard of deepwater sea fans and tube sponges.

The color orange is prevalent, from grapefruit-sized orange ball sponges, which dot the reef like orange speckles, to the feathery arms of orange crinoids that reach out of the crevices. The heavy folds of orange elephant ear sponges also help raise the level of orangeness to noticeable proportions.

Location: 3 nautical miles (5.7km) NNE of Loggerhead Key

Depth Range: Surface-50ft (15m)

Access: Boat or live-aboard

Expertise Rating: Intermediate

This site is often swept in moderate currents. Schools of horse-eye jacks and great barracuda circle in the water col-

A stoplight parrotfish lounges on an elephant ear sponge.

umn adjacent to the reef, while a variety of parrotfish, wrasses and angelfish stick close to the corals. If you have an eye for smaller creatures, you'll also find a wide range of goby and blenny species at Texas Rock.

60 Fort Jefferson Moat Wall

The outer face of the moat wall surrounding Fort Jefferson is a splendid snorkeling site. Scuba is not recommended, as depths are only 3 to 6ft. Entry is from the beach beside the campsites. The bottom is mostly sand and seagrass with scattered coral patches, and the water gets progressively deeper as you swim away from the wall. Several hundred yards out are some nice patch reefs in 15 to 20ft of water, but stay clear of the boat channels leading to the Garden Key anchorage. The best snorkeling is in the shallows, which spar buoys mark off as no-boating zones.

Location: Garden Key

Depth Range: Surface-20ft (6m)

Access: Boat, live-aboard or seaplane to Fort Jefferson; shore from fort

Expertise Rating: Novice

Beside the wall and along the brickwork itself is where you'll find all the action. Expect to come across almost anything, from Caribbean octopuses and pencil urchins to sea anemones and yellow stingrays. The hard corals are represented mostly by small heads of star and brain coral, but there are plenty of healthy sea fans and sea plumes. Stoplight parrotfish, porkfish and bluestriped grunts dominate the fish population, while starry-eyed hermit crabs and queen conch are also plentiful.

Circumnavigating the fort with snorkel and fins is a fascinating adventure. Watch for boat traffic near the dock and a short stretch beside the channel, but the rest of the route is clear. Sand shoals now block the channel adjacent to the old coal dock to all traffic except very small boats. The pilings of the old dock are coated with sponges and corals and packed with fish, including huge tarpon. Although they can weigh close to 100 pounds, tarpon are not a danger to divers or snorkelers.

After you tour Fort Jeff, snorkel the outer face of the moat wall.

61 Windjammer

Also known as the French Wreck, this 261ft iron-hulled sailing vessel was built in Scotland in 1875. Originally named *Killean*, then *Antonin* and finally *Avanti*, she lost her rudder and ran aground on Loggerhead Reef in 1907 while carrying lumber from Pensacola to South America. All 32 crewmen were lost in the tragic wreck.

Location: 1 nautical mile (1.9km) SW of Loggerhead Key

Depth Range: Surface-18ft (6m)

Access: Boat or live-aboard

Expertise Rating: Novice

The maximum depth at this site is only 18ft, and parts of the wreck are exposed at low tide. The bow section has been flattened by the sea, but is still mostly intact, with the graceful bowsprit still attached. The hull is densely covered with healthy spheres of star and brain coral, one mound heaped upon the other. Schools of Bermuda chub sweep ceaselessly back and forth, winding in and out among the corals.

The ship's structure is open amidships, where it broke apart during the grounding. A section of one of the tall masts remains fastened to the vessel, but now rests flat on the sand. Several tiger groupers and two large jewfish reside within the hull.

The stern section lies on the sand a short swim from the bow. A trail of plating and broken rigging leads from one section to the other. The stern is more broken up than the bow, but still provides excellent habitat for fish, including hundreds of yellow goatfish and mangrove snappers.

The Windjammer is an excellent wreck for snorkelers, but photographers will probably prefer scuba. A single mooring buoy bobs between the two sections.

Dense mounds of star and brain coral shroud the wreck.

Marine Life

The Florida Keys are home to nearly all of the marine species found throughout The Bahamas and Caribbean, thanks to the influence of the Gulf Stream. Surveys in the region have identified more than 500 fish species, 63 hard-coral species, 42 soft-coral species, 82 species of echinoderms and 38 species of sponges. This incredible diversity is matched by sheer numbers, following many years of marine park and sanctuary protection.

Though it would be impractical to list all the species you are likely to see while diving in the Keys, this section will identify some of the more common vertebrates and invertebrates. The next section describes potentially harmful or dangerous marine life you might encounter.

Keep in mind that common names are used freely by most divers and are often inconsistent. The two-part scientific name is more precise. This system is known as binomial nomenclature—the method of using two words (shown in italics) to identify an organism. The first italic word is the genus, into which members of similar species are grouped. The second word, the species, refers to a recognizable group within a genus whose members are capable of interbreeding.

Common Vertebrates

squirrelfish
Holocentrus ascensionis

trumpetfish
Aulostomus maculatus

jewfish
Epinephelus itajara

coney
Cephalopholis fulva

butter hamlet
Hypoplectrus unicolor

redspotted hawkfish
Amblycirrhitus pinos

snook
Centropomus undecimalis

horse-eye jack
Caranx latus

schoolmaster
Lutjanus apodus

porkfish
Anisotremus virginicus

French grunt
Haemulon flavolineatum

spotted drum
Equetus punctatus

yellow goatfish
Mulloidichthys martinicus

Atlantic spadefish
Chaetodipterus faber

foureye butterflyfish
Chaetodon capistratus

rock beauty
Holacanthus tricolor

queen angelfish
Holacanthus ciliaris

sergeant major
Abudefduf saxatilis

Spanish hogfish (juvenile)
Bodianus rufus

stoplight parrotfish (male)
Sparisoma viride

yellowhead jawfish
Opistognathus aurifrons

saddled blenny
Malacoctenus triangulatus

neon goby
Gobiosoma oceanops

blue tang (juvenile)
Acanthurus coeruleus

whitespotted filefish (orange phase)
Cantherhines macrocerus

balloonfish
Diodon holocanthus

hawksbill turtle
Eretmochelys imbricata

Common Invertebrates

strawberry vase sponge
Mycale laxissima

common sea fan
Gorgonia ventalina

great star coral
Montastraea cavernosa

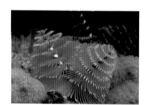

Christmas tree worm
Spirobranchus giganteus

flamingo tongue
Cyphoma gibbosum

reef squid
Sepioteuthis sepioidea

spiny lobster
Panulirus argus

banded coral shrimp
Stenopus hispidus

channel clinging crab
Mithrax spinosissimus

Hazardous Marine Life

Marine animals almost never attack divers, but many have defensive and offensive weaponry that can be triggered if they feel threatened or annoyed. The ability to recognize hazardous creatures is a valuable asset in avoiding injury. Following are some of the potentially hazardous creatures most commonly found in the Keys.

Fire Coral

Although often mistaken for stony coral, fire coral is a hydroid colony that secretes a hard, calcareous skeleton. Fire coral grows in many different shapes, often encrusting or taking the form of a variety of reef structures. It is usually identifiable by its tan, mustard or brown color and finger-like columns with whitish tips. The entire colony is covered by tiny pores and fine, hair-like projections nearly invisible to the unaided eye. To avoid injury, simply steer clear. Fire coral "stings" by discharging small, specialized cells called nematocysts. Contact causes a burning sensation that lasts for several minutes and may produce red welts on the skin. Do not rub the area, as you will only spread the stinging particles. Cortisone cream can reduce the inflammation, and antihistamine cream is good for killing the pain. Serious stings should be treated by a doctor.

Bristle Worm

Also called fire worms, bristle worms are found among reef rubble and seagrass beds. They have segmented bodies covered with either tufts or bundles of sensory hairs that extend in tiny, sharp, detachable bristles. If you touch one, the tiny stinging bristles lodge in your skin and cause a burning sensation that may be followed by a red spot or welt. Remove embedded bristles with adhesive tape, rubber cement or a commercial facial peel. Apply a decontaminant such as vinegar, rubbing alcohol or dilute ammonia.

Jellyfish

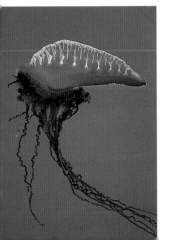

Jellyfish sting by releasing the stinging cells contained in their trailing tentacles. As a rule, the longer the tentacles, the more painful the sting. Three species of jellyfish are common in the Keys: the Portuguese man-o-war (*Physalia physalis*), the moon jelly (*Aurelia aurita*) and the mangrove upside-down jelly (*Cassiopea xamachana*). The man-o-war (see photo) is the most toxic, with large tentacles that may trail far below its floating body. Moon jellies grow as large as dinner plates and are most often encountered in the late summer and fall.

123

Their tentacles are very short, and they are not potent stingers, but a strong current can sometimes sweep large numbers of them over a reef. They tend to hover in mid-water or near the surface, so be on the lookout as you ascend from a dive. Upside-down jellies are frequently found in shallow water, especially in Florida Bay. You can see them on the bottom, with their short tentacles facing up. Stings are often irritating and not painful, but should be treated immediately with a decontaminant such as vinegar, rubbing alcohol, baking soda, papain or dilute household ammonia. Beware that some people may have a stronger reaction than others, in which case you should prepare to resuscitate and seek medical aid.

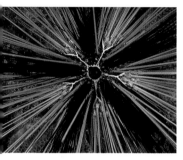

Sea Urchin

Sea urchins live in shallow areas near shore and come out of their shelters at night. They vary in coloration and size, with spines ranging from short and blunt to long and needle-sharp. The spines are the urchin's most dangerous weapon, easily able to penetrate neoprene wetsuits, booties and gloves. Treat minor punctures by extracting the spines and immersing the area in nonscalding hot water. More serious injuries require medical attention.

Scorpionfish

Scorpionfish are well-camouflaged creatures that have poisonous spines along their dorsal fins. They are often difficult to spot, since they typically rest quietly on the bottom or on coral, looking more like rocks. Practice good buoyancy control and watch where you put your hands. Scorpionfish wounds can be excruciating. To treat a puncture, wash the wound and immerse it in nonscalding hot water for 30 to 90 minutes.

Moray Eel

Distinguished by their long, thick, snake-like bodies and tapered heads, moray eels come in a variety of colors and patterns. Don't feed them or put your hand in a dark hole—eels have the unfortunate combination of sharp teeth and poor eyesight and will bite if they feel threatened. If you are bitten, don't try to pull your hand away suddenly—the eel's teeth slant backward and are extraordinarily sharp. Let the eel release it and then surface slowly. Treat with antiseptics, anti-tetanus and antibiotics.

Barracuda

Barracuda are identifiable by their long, silver, cylindrical bodies and razor-like teeth protruding from an underslung jaw. They swim alone or in small groups, continually opening and closing their mouths, an action that looks daunting but actually assists their respiration. Though bar-

racuda will hover near divers to observe, they are really somewhat shy, though they may be attracted by shiny objects that resemble fishing lures. Irrigate a barracuda bite with fresh water and treat with antiseptics, anti-tetanus and antibiotics.

Shark

Sharks come in many shapes and sizes. They are most recognizable by their triangular dorsal fin. Though many species are shy, such as the nurse shark (see photo), there are occasional attacks, albeit rarely in the Keys. About 25 species worldwide are considered dangerous to humans. Sharks will generally not attack unless provoked, so don't taunt, tease or feed them. Avoid spearfishing, carrying fish baits or mimicking a wounded fish and your likelihood of being attacked will greatly diminish. Face and quietly watch any shark that is acting aggressively and be prepared to push it away with a camera, knife or tank. If someone is bitten by a shark, stop the bleeding, reassure the patient, treat for shock and seek immediate medical aid.

Stingray

Identified by its diamond-shaped body and wide "wings," the stingray has one or two venomous spines at the base of its tail. Stingrays like shallow waters and tend to rest on silty or sandy bottoms, often burying themselves in the sand. Often only the eyes, gill slits and tail are visible. These creatures are harmless

unless you sit or step on them. Though injuries are uncommon, wounds are always extremely painful and often deep and infective. Immerse wound in non-scalding hot water and seek medical aid.

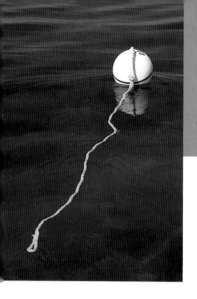

Diving Conservation & Awareness

The name Pennekamp is synonymous with marine conservation in the Florida Keys. John Pennekamp, longtime editor of *The Miami Herald*, and many others were indeed instrumental in establishing a true marine park and raising awareness of the need for conservation. But the story of marine conservation in the Keys goes much further. An overlapping networks of parks, refuges and sanctuaries has been established over the years, each zone working in concert with its neighbors to protect the region's natural and historic resources.

Marine Reserves & Regulations

Fort Jefferson National Monument was the first park, securing protection for the historic fort and surrounding waters in 1935. The park was renamed Dry Tortugas National Park in 1992. The next part of the coral reef ecosystem to be protected was the Everglades, which provides nursery grounds for many species and is an important source of fresh water. Everglades National Park was designated in 1947.

The reefs themselves, though, were pillaged for shells, tropical fish and coral in the 1950s, prompting creation of John Pennekamp Coral Reef State Park in 1960.

The Keys' first park was Fort Jefferson in the Dry Tortugas, where reefs are widely protected.

The original park was about 20 miles (32km) long and stretched from the shoreline out to a depth of 60ft (18m), approximately 5 miles (8km) offshore. A U.S. Supreme Court ruling on another matter later reduced the state of Florida's jurisdiction to 3 miles (4.8km) offshore, leaving most of the reefs unprotected. The Key Largo National Marine Sanctuary was quickly designated to correct the problem, and coral reef protection off Key Largo now extends seamlessly from the shore to a depth of 300ft (91m). Looe Key National Marine Sanctuary was set aside in 1981, bringing coral reef management to the Middle Keys.

In 1989 a series of ship groundings destroyed acres of coral, and officials realized the need for a more comprehensive management plan. Congress created the Florida Keys National Marine Sanctuary (FKNMS) the following year and tasked the National Oceanic and Atmospheric Administration (NOAA) with developing a plan. The FKNMS sanctuary plan was approved five years later, significantly spreading the umbrella of protection.

Sanctuary Regulations

Diving etiquette is largely common sense: Enjoy yourself, but don't damage the coral. Following is a summary of the rules pertaining to divers and snorkelers within the Florida Keys National Marine Sanctuary; check with the sanctuary or the Florida Marine Patrol for the complete regulations:

- Do not touch, stand on, kick, break or remove coral.
- Do not remove, damage or disturb scientific equipment or historical artifacts.
- Do not run aground on the reefs or injure seagrass with your boat.
- Do not anchor in coral or allow your anchor chain or line to contact coral.
- Display a dive flag when diving or snorkeling.
- Operate at idle speed within 100 yards (91m) of dive flags, stationary vessels, residential shorelines and navigational aids marking shallow reefs.
- Access to refuge areas may be restricted to nonmotorized vessels, idle speed only or by season. Some areas may be closed to access altogether.

That plan in turn focused attention on water quality issues now being addressed by the state of Florida, Monroe County and the U.S. Environmental Protection Agency (EPA). Vital programs such as a countywide sewer system to replace existing septic tanks will make a tremendous difference in the long-term health of the reefs.

An FKNMS zoning plan initiated in 1997 safeguards certain sensitive or high-use areas. Eighteen sanctuary preservation areas (SPAs) protect the most popular diving reefs, creating no-harvest and no-disturbance zones. Also protected are 15 existing management areas under the Florida Department of Environmental Protection, four U.S. Fish and Wildlife Service refuges and two ecological reserves devoted to marine life replenishment.

The big question: Does protection work? The answer: yes and no.

No, because live coral cover continues to decline. The primary causes are coral disease and bleaching, which are exacerbated by global warming, pollution,

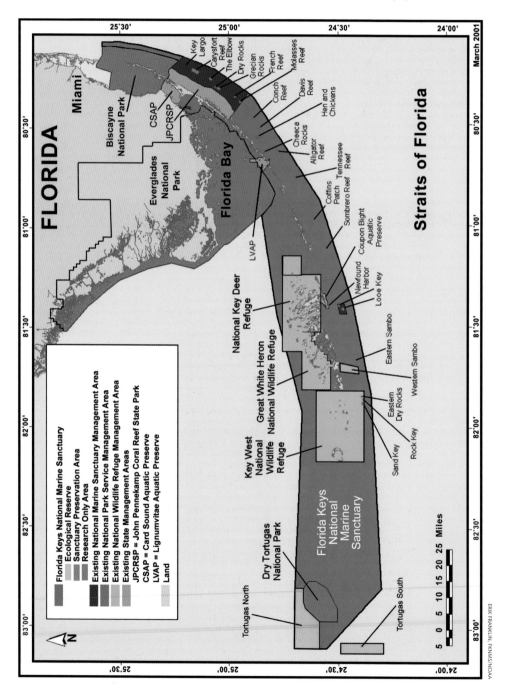

Black-band disease is an algal infestation that spreads across a coral, killing polyps in its wake.

sedimentation, turbidity and changes in salinity. Most, perhaps all, of those factors are due to human impact. Each of us creates several pounds of trash and garbage and many gallons of wastewater a day. In the Keys there are also point and non-point sources of pollution such as farming, fuel combustion and storm drains. Other reasons for the decline are directly linked to diving and snorkeling, including damage from boat groundings and contact from dive fins and tanks. In the last decade vessel groundings alone have destroyed nearly 20 acres (8 hectares) of coral reef habitat and damaged thousands of acres of seagrass.

But the answer is also yes, for two reasons. First, the coral reefs are in much better condition today than they might have been, thanks to the last 40 years of conservation and management. Second, the umbrella of marine protection is making a difference for the future. Fish populations are increasing within the protected zones, efforts are being made to reduce excess nutrients and contaminants in wastewater and runoff, and we are diving with more respect and care.

Responsible Diving

Dive sites are often along reefs and walls covered in beautiful corals and sponges. It only takes a moment—an inadvertently placed hand or knee, or a careless brush or kick with a fin—to destroy this fragile, living part of our delicate ecosystem. By following these basic guidelines while diving, you can help preserve the ecology and beauty of the reefs:

1. Never drop boat anchors onto a coral reef, and take care not to ground boats on coral.

Mooring 101

Designed by marine biologist John Halas (see photo), the mooring buoys in the Florida Keys National Marine Sanctuary not only save the reefs from anchor damage, they save you time and effort. Finding the site you want is easier and tying up to a buoy is a snap.

More than one boat can tie up to a single mooring in tandem, if sea and wind conditions permit and all the vessel captains agree. The moorings are available on a "first come, first served" basis, regardless of whether the boat is commercial or private. If a boat is waiting for the mooring you are occupying, however, as a courtesy you should move as soon as practical after your dive.

The moorings are marked with letters and numbers. The letters indicate the reef, as in M for Molasses or NN for North North Dry Rocks. The numbers, from 1 to the maximum number of moorings on that particular reef, indicate specific dive sites. Every attempt is made to keep the buoys in the same numerical order on each reef, but they may temporarily be in different positions.

About 400 moorings have been installed in the Keys. The sanctuary and its contractors do an excellent job of keeping them maintained, but you can help. Avoid running over the pickup lines or colliding with the floats. If problems are encountered, notify the mooring buoy hot line at 305-852-7717, ext. 45.

2. Practice and maintain proper buoyancy control and avoid overweighting. Be aware that buoyancy can change over the period of an extended trip. Initially you may breathe harder and need more weighting; a few days later you may breathe more easily and need less weight. Tip: Use your weight belt and tank position to maintain a horizontal position—raise them to elevate your feet, lower them to elevate your upper body. Also be careful about buoyancy loss: As you go deeper, your wetsuit compresses, as does the air in your BC.

3. Avoid touching living marine organisms with your body and equipment. Polyps can be damaged by even the gentlest contact. Never stand on or touch living coral. The use of gloves is not recommended: Gloves make it too easy to hold on to the reef, damaging the coral. Steady yourself in the sand or, if you must touch the reef, use only your fingertips on dead coral.

4. Take great care in underwater caves. Spend as little time within them as possible, as your air bubbles can damage fragile organisms. Divers should take turns inspecting the interiors of small caves or under ledges to lessen the chances of damaging contact.

5. Be conscious of your fins. Even without contact, the surge from heavy fin strokes near the reef can do damage. Avoid full-leg kicks when diving close to the bottom and when leaving a photo scene. When you inadvertently kick something, stop kicking! It seems obvious, but some divers either panic or are totally oblivious when they bump something. When treading water in shallow reef areas, take care not to kick up clouds of sand. Settling sand can smother the delicate reef organisms.

6. Secure gauges, computer consoles and the octopus regulator so they're not dangling—they are like miniature wrecking balls to a reef.

7. When swimming in strong currents, be extra careful about leg kicks and handholds.

8. Photographers should take extra precautions, as cameras and equipment affect buoyancy. Changing f-stops, framing a subject and maintaining position for a photo often conspire to thwart the ideal "no-touch" approach on a reef. When you must use "holdfasts," choose them intelligently (e.g., use one finger only for leverage off an area of dead coral).

9. Resist the temptation to collect or buy coral or shells. Aside from the ecological damage, collection of marine souvenirs depletes the beauty of a site and spoils other divers' enjoyment.

10. Ensure that you take home all your trash and any litter you may find as well. Plastics in particular pose a serious threat to marine life.

11. Resist the temptation to feed fish. You may disturb their normal eating habits, encourage aggressive behavior or feed them food that is detrimental to their health.

12. Minimize your disturbance of marine animals. Don't ride on the backs of turtles, as this can cause them great anxiety.

Marine Conservation Organizations

Coral reefs and oceans face unprecedented environmental pressures. The following groups are actively involved in promoting responsible diving, publicizing environmental marine threats and lobbying for better policies. (See Listings, page 140, for more info.)

CORAL: The Coral Reef Alliance
☎ 510-848-0110
www.coral.org

Ocean Futures
☎ 805-899-8899
www.oceanfutures.com

Cousteau Society
☎ 757-523-9335
www.cousteausociety.org

ReefKeeper International
☎ 305-358-4600
www.reefkeeper.org

Project AWARE Foundation
☎ 714-540-0251
www.projectaware.org

Reef Relief
☎ 305-294-3100
www.reefrelief.org

Listings

Telephone Calls

If you are calling within the U.S., dial 1 + 305 + the local 7-digit number. Toll-free numbers can be accessed from the U.S. and, usually, Canada: dial 1 + the area code (800, 866, 877 or 888) + the 7-digit toll-free number.

Diving Services

Don't expect that your hotel, dive shop and dive boat will all be at the same location. That happy circumstance is only true for a few of the dive operations in the Keys. Typically, your dive shop will be on U.S. 1 and its boat in a nearby canal or marina. Hotel pickup service is not offered.

Most of the operators listed below offer morning and afternoon trips each day. Both are usually two-tank trips. Almost every shop also schedules at least one night dive per week. Additional night dives can be arranged, but normally a minimum of four to six divers will be required.

Tips for Evaluating a Dive Operator

Everyone has their own preferences when it comes to a dive operator, but we all expect some basics, like safety, efficiency and fun. How do you make sure that's what you'll get? Here are some things to look for:

- Is the operation well organized? Is signup quick and easy? The best dive operators take you through all the necessary procedures with minimum effort, but don't make you feel like you're on an assembly line.

- Check out the customer amenities. Is parking convenient? Is a comfortable area provided while you wait to board the dive boat? Does the operation have a retail store, and does it stock the gear you might need? Are snacks and beverages available for the trip? Is there a clean gear-rinse and storage area?

- Careful maintenance is a promising sign. Are the facilities in good condition? Is the rental gear well maintained and carefully stored? Is the dive boat clean and reliable?

- Take a peek at the compressor room. Is it well ventilated and clean? Are the tanks in good shape?

- Find out how long the staff has worked there. Staff longevity is good, as it means people are well treated and enjoying their jobs.

- Is everyone having fun? If the customers and staff are having a good time, you probably will too.

Tanks, weights and weight belts are provided for each trip. Eighty-cubic-foot (2,265-liter) aluminum tanks are most commonly used, though 62s (1,755-liter) may be available if requested ahead of time. Almost all tanks in the Keys are fitted with K-valves for yoke-style (also called A-clamp) regulators. Some shops have adapters for DIN regulators, but you shouldn't count on it unless you make advance arrangements.

The Florida Keys may have the best selection of rental and retail dive gear in the world. The dive operators here get the good stuff, and many of them replace it every year with new gear. If you show up with only your certification card, almost any shop in the Keys can have you fully outfitted in 10 minutes.

Many of the operators listed belong to the Keys Association of Dive Operators. KADO was established to ensure professionalism among dive operators and protect the reef through safe boating and ecologically sound diving practices. The organization has also been instrumental in sinking several ships as alternate dive sites. For more information, including a list of members, visit the KADO website at www.divekeys.com.

Key Biscayne

Divers Unlimited
Convoy Point Visitor's Center
Biscayne National Park
9710 SW 328th St.

Homestead, FL 33033
☎ 230-1100
www.nps.gov/bisc/visit/concession.htm
dive970@aol.com

Upper Keys

Admiral Dive Center
MM 105
P.O. Box 0113
Key Largo, FL 33037
toll-free ☎ 800-346-3483
☎ 451-1114 fax: 451-2731
www.admiralcenter.com
admiral@admiralcenter.com

Amoray Dive Resort
MM 104.25
104250 Overseas Highway
Key Largo, FL 33037
toll-free ☎ 800-426-6729
☎ 451-3595 fax: 453-9516
www.amoray.com
amoraydive@aol.com

Aqua-Nut Divers
MM 104.2
104220 Overseas Highway
Key Largo, FL 33037

toll-free ☎ 800-226-0415
☎ 451-1622 fax: 451-4623
www.aqua-nuts.com
info@aqua-nuts.com

Atlantis Dive Center
MM 106.5
51 Garden Cove Drive
Key Largo, FL 33037
toll-free ☎ 800-331-3483
☎ 451-3020 fax: 451-9240
www.captainslate.com
dive@captainslate.com

Caribbean Watersports
MM 97
P.O. Box 781
Key Largo, FL 33037
toll-free ☎ 800-223-6728
☎ 664-9547 fax: 664-4015
www.caribbeanwatersports.com
cwsports@aol.com

Upper Keys (continued)

Conch Republic Divers
MM 90.8
90800 Overseas Highway, #9
Tavernier, FL 33037
toll-free ☎ 800-274-3483
☎ 852-1655 fax: 853-0031
www.conchrepublicdivers.com
dive@conchrepublicdivers.com

Divers City USA
MM 104
104001 Overseas Highway
Key Largo, FL 33037
toll-free ☎ 800-649-4659
☎ 451-4554 fax: 451-5251
www.diverscityusa.com
mail@diverscityusa.com

Florida Keys Dive Center
MM 90.5
P.O. Box 391
Tavernier, FL 33070
toll-free ☎ 800-433-8946
☎ 852-4599 fax: 852-1293
www.floridakeysdivectr.com
scuba@floridakeysdivectr.com

Holiday Isle Dive Shop
MM 84.5
P.O. Box 482
Islamorada, FL 33036
toll-free ☎ 800-327-7070, ext. 644
☎ 664-3483 ☎/fax: 664-4145
www.divetheisle.com
diveshop@divetheisle.com

Island Reef Diver
MM 99.5
3 Seagate Blvd.
Key Largo, FL 33037
☎ 453-9456 fax: 453-9405
www.islandreefdiver.com
isldiver@bellsouth.net

It's a Dive Island Adventures
MM 80
80001 Overseas Highway
Islamorada, FL 33036
toll-free ☎ 866-664-0095
☎ 664-0095 fax: 664-8775
www.itsadive2.com
info@itsadive2.com

It's a Dive Watersports
MM 103.8
103800 Overseas Highway
Key Largo, FL 33037
toll-free ☎ 800-809-9881
☎ 453-9881 fax: 451-4350
www.itsadive.com
info@itsadive.com

John Pennekamp Coral Reef State Park Dive Shop
MM 102.5
P.O. Box 1560
Key Largo, FL 33037
toll-free ☎ 877-538-7348
☎ 451-6322 fax: 451-6309
www.pennekamppark.com
jpcrsp@terranova.net

Jules' Undersea Lodge
Key Largo Undersea Park
MM 103.2
51 Shoreland Drive
Key Largo, FL 33037
☎ 451-2353 fax: 451-4789
www.jul.com
info@jul.com

Keys Diver
MM 100
99696 Overseas Highway, #1
Key Largo, FL 33037
toll-free ☎ 888-289-2402
☎ 451-1177 fax: 451-6389
www.keysdiver.com
tbfirm@aol.com

Lady Cyana Divers
MM 85.9
P.O. Box 1157
Islamorada, FL 33036
toll-free ☎ 800-221-8717
☎ 664-8717 fax: 664-4443
www.ladycyana.com
ladycyana@ladycyana.com

Ocean Divers
MM 100
522 Caribbean Drive
Key Largo, FL 33037
toll-free ☎ 800-451-1113
☎ 451-1113 fax: 451-5765
www.oceandivers.com
info@oceandivers.com

Upper Keys (continued)

Ocean Quest Dive Center
MM 85.5
85500 Overseas Highway
Islamorada, FL 33036
toll-free ☎ 800-356-8798
☎ 664-4401
www.oceanquestdivecenter.com
mail@oceanquestdivecenter.com

Quiescence Diving Services
MM 103.5
P.O. Box 1570
Key Largo, FL 33037
☎ 451-2440 fax: 451-6440
www.keylargodiving.com
www.quiescence.com
info@keylargodiving.com

Rainbow Reef Dive Center
MM 84.9
P.O. Box 153
Islamorada, FL 33036
toll-free ☎ 800-457-4354
☎ 664-4600 fax: 664-2007
www.rainbowreef-divecenter.com
divers@rainbowreef-divecenter.com

Scuba-Do Diving Charters
MM 100
522 Caribbean Drive
Key Largo, FL 33037
toll-free ☎ 800-516-0110
☎ 451-3446 fax: 853-0950
cell: 522-1271
www.scuba-do.com
dive@scuba-do.com

Sea Dwellers Dive Center
MM 100
99050 Overseas Highway
Key Largo, FL 33037
toll-free ☎ 800-451-3640
☎ 451-3640 fax: 451-1935
www.sea-dwellers.com
sdwellers@aol.com

Sharky's Dive Center
MM 100
Holiday Inn Marina
106240 Overseas Highway
Key Largo, FL 33037

toll-free ☎ 800-935-3483
☎ 451-5533 fax: 451-0124
sharkys@scubanetwork.com

Silent World Dive Center
MM 103.2
P.O. Box 2363
Key Largo, FL 33037
toll-free ☎ 800-966-3483
☎/fax: 451-3252
www.silentworldkeylargo.com
info@silentworldkeylargo.com

Sundiver Station Snorkel Shop
MM 103
102840 Overseas Highway
Key Largo, FL 33037
toll-free ☎ 800-453-9386 or
   800-654-7369
☎ 451-2220 fax: 451-1211
www.sundiverstation.com

Tavernier Dive Center
MM 90.7
P.O. Box 465
Tavernier, FL 33070
toll-free ☎ 800-787-9797
☎ 852-4007 fax: 852-0869
www.tavernierdivecenter.com
tavdive@tavernierdivecenter.com

Upper Keys Dive & Sport Center
MM 90.5
90701 Old Highway
Tavernier, FL 33070
toll-free ☎ 800-537-3253
☎ 852-8799 fax: 852-4605
http://florida-keys.fl.us/upperkeysdive
upperkeysdive@florida-keys.fl.us

Wreck Diver Ventures
MM 103.2
P.O. Box 401
Key Largo, FL 33037
toll-free ☎ 877-299-3483
☎/fax: 451-3900
www.wreckdiverventures.com
wrkdiver@gate.net

Middle Keys

Abyss Dive Center
MM 54
Holiday Inn Marina
13175 Overseas Highway
Marathon, FL 33050
toll-free ☎ 800-457-0134
☎ 743-2126 fax: 743-7081
www.abyssdive.com
info@abyssdive.com

Aquatic Adventures Dive Center
MM 54
P.O. Box 510378
Key Colony Beach, FL 33051
toll-free ☎ 800-978-3483
☎/fax: 743-2421
www.aaquaticadventure.com
aqautic@aaquaticadventure.com

Capt. Hook's Dive Center
MM 53
11833 Overseas Highway
Marathon, FL 33050
toll-free ☎ 800-278-4665
☎ 743-2444 fax: 289-1374
www.captainhooks.com
info@captainhooks.com

The Diving Site
MM 53.5
12399 Overseas Highway
Marathon, FL 33050
toll-free ☎ 800-634-3935
☎ 289-1021 fax: 289-0046
www.divingsite.com
diving@divingsite.com

Fantasea Divers
MM 49.5
4650 Overseas Highway
Marathon, FL 33050

toll-free ☎ 800-223-4563
☎ 743-5422 fax: 743-4739
www.thefloridakeys.com/fantasea
divenxs@aol.com

Hall's Diving Center
MM 48.5
1994 Overseas Highway
Marathon, FL 33050
toll-free ☎ 800-331-4255
☎ 743-5929 fax: 743-8168
www.hallsdiving.com
request@hallsdiving.com

Marathon Divers & Sports Center
MM 53.5
12221 Overseas Highway
Marathon, FL 33050
toll-free ☎ 800-724-5798
☎ 289-1141
www.marathondivers.com
info@marathondivers.com

Middle Keys Scuba Center
MM 52.8
11511 Overseas Highway
Marathon, FL 33050
☎/fax: 743-2902
www.divingdiscovery.com
rboileau@aol.com

Sombrero Reef Explorers
19 Sombrero Blvd.
Marathon, FL 33050
☎ 743-0536
www.sombreroreef.com
captfred@sombreroreef.com

Lower Keys & Key West

Bonsai Diving
1075 Duval St., C-9
Key West, FL 33040
☎ 296-6301 ☎/fax: 294-2921
www.bonsaidiving.com
divekw@aol.com

Florida Keys Reef-Divers
MM 21
477 Drost Drive
Cudjoe Key, FL 33042
☎ 745-2357 fax: 744-0533
www.reef-divers.com
jim@reef-divers.com

Lower Keys & Key West (continued)

Dive Key West
3128 N. Roosevelt Blvd.
Key West, FL 33040
toll-free ☎ 800-426-0707
☎ 296-3823 fax: 296-0609
www.divekeywest.com
info@divekeywest.com

Get Wet
509 Duval St.
Key West, FL 33040
toll-free ☎ 877-276-6755
☎ 294-7738 fax: 295-9755
www.discountkeywest.com

Innerspace Dive Center
MM 29.5
P.O. Box 430651
Big Pine Key, FL 33043
toll-free ☎ 800-538-2896
☎ 872-2319 fax: 872-3081
diveinnerspace@aol.com

Key West Diving Society
MM 4.5
5110 Overseas Highway
Key West, FL 33040
☎ 292-3221 fax: 294-7177
www.keywestdivingsociety.com
kwds@keysconnection.com

Looe Key Reef Resort & Dive Center
MM 27.5
P.O. Box 509
Ramrod Key, FL 33042
toll-free ☎ 800-942-5397
☎ 872-2215 fax: 872-3786
www.diveflakeys.com
looekeydiv@aol.com

Lost Reef Adventures
261 Margaret St.
Key West, FL 33040
toll-free ☎ 800-952-2749
☎ 296-9737 fax: 296-6660
www.lostreefadventures.com
lostreefkw@aol.com

Paradise Divers
MM 39
38801 Overseas Highway
Big Pine Key, FL 33043
☎ 872-1114 fax: 872-5430
www.paradivers.com
paradivers@aol.com

Sea Breeze Reef Raiders
617 Front St.
Key West, FL 33040
toll-free ☎ 800-370-7745
☎ 292-7745 fax: 292-7725
www.keywestscubadive.com
seabreezecharters@flakeysol.com

Southpoint Divers
714 Duval St.
Key West, FL 33040
toll-free ☎ 800-891-3483
☎ 292-9778 fax: 296-6888
www.southpointdivers.com
southpoint@aol.com

Strike Zone Charters
MM 29.5
29675 Overseas Highway
Big Pine Key, FL 33043
toll-free ☎ 800-654-9560
☎ 872-9863 fax: 872-0520
www.strikezonecharter.com
strizone@aol.com

Subtropic Dive Center
1605 N. Roosevelt Blvd.
Key West, FL 33040
toll-free ☎ 800-853-3483
☎ 296-9914 fax: 296-9918
www.subtropic.com
info@subtropic.com

Underseas
MM 30.5
P.O. Box 430319
Big Pine Key, FL 33043
toll-free ☎ 800-446-5663
☎ 872-2700 fax: 872-0080
www.keysdirectory.com/underseas
diveuseas@aol.com

Public Boat Ramps

Barnes Sound,
MM 110 bayside

John Pennekamp Coral Reef State Park,
MM102.5 oceanside

Sunset Point,
MM 95.2 bayside

Community Harbor,
MM 92 bayside

Harry Harris Park,
MM 92.5 oceanside

Indian Key Fill,
MM 78.8 bayside

Marathon,
MM 54 bayside

Marathon,
MM 49 bayside

Seven Mile Bridge,
MM 40 bayside

Bahia Honda State Park,
MM 37 oceanside

Spanish Harbor,
MM 34 bayside

Cudjoe Key,
MM 20 bayside

Big Coppitt Key,
MM 11 oceanside

Stock Island,
MM 5.2 oceanside

Simonton Street,
Key West Harbor, Key West

Smathers Beach,
S. Roosevelt Blvd., Key West

Garrison Bight,
N. Roosevelt Blvd., Key West

Live-Aboards

Sea-Clusive Charters
P.O. Box 431961
Big Pine Key, FL 33043
☎ 744-9928 fax: 745-4311
www.seaclusive.com
seaclusivekw@aol.com

Taylor Made Excursions
P.O. Box 6556
Key West, FL 33041
☎ 293-9183
www.scubaworld.com/taylormade
taylormade@scubaworld.com

State Parks

Bahia Honda State Park
MM 37
36850 Overseas Highway
Big Pine Key, FL 33043
☎ 872-2353

Curry Hammock State Park
MM 56.2
Marathon
☎ 664-4815

**Fort Zachary Taylor Historic
State Park**
P.O. Box 6560

Key West, FL 33041
☎ 292-6713

Indian Key Historic State Park
MM 78.5
P.O. Box 1052
Islamorada, FL 33036
☎ 664-2540

**John Pennekamp Coral Reef
State Park**
MM 102.5
P.O. Box 487
Key Largo, FL 33037
☎ 451-1202

Key Largo Hammocks Botanical
State Park
County Road 905
P.O. Box 487
Key Largo, FL 33037
☎ 451-1202

Lignumvitae Key Botanical
State Park
MM 78.5
P.O. Box 1052
Islamorada, FL 33036
☎ 664-2540

Long Key State Park
MM 67.5
P.O. Box 776

Long Key, FL 33001
☎ 664-4815

San Pedro Underwater Archeological
Preserve State Park
P.O. Box 1052
Islamorada, FL 33036
☎ 664-2540

Windley Key Fossil Reef Geological
State Park
P.O. Box 1052
Islamorada, FL 33036
☎ 664-2540

Chambers of Commerce

You'll find comprehensive listings for accommodations and restaurants throughout the Florida Keys and Key West on the official Monroe County Tourist Development Council website at www.fla-keys.com. Contact information for individual chambers of commerce is listed below in order from north to south:

Key Largo Chamber of Commerce
MM 106
106000 Overseas Highway
Key Largo, FL 33037
toll-free ☎ 800-822-1088
☎ 451-1414 or 4747 fax: 451-4726
www.keylargo.org
klchamber@aol.com

Islamorada Chamber of Commerce
MM 82.5
P.O. Box 915
Islamorada, FL 33036
toll-free ☎ 800-322-5397
☎ 664-4503 fax: 664-4289
www.islamoradachamber.com
info@islamoradachamber.com

Greater Marathon
    Chamber of Commerce
MM 53.5
12222 Overseas Highway
Marathon, FL 33050

toll-free ☎ 800-842-9580 or
    800-262-7284
☎ 743-5417 fax: 289-0183
www.floridakeysmarathon.com
marathoncc@aol.com

Lower Keys Chamber of Commerce
MM 31
P.O. Box 430511
Big Pine Key, FL 33043-0511
toll-free ☎ 800-872-3722
☎ 872-2411 fax: 872-0752
www.lowerkeyschamber.com
lkchamber@aol.com

Key West Chamber of Commerce
402 Wall St.
Key West, FL 33040
toll-free ☎ 800-527-8539
☎ 294-2587 fax: 294-7806
www.keywestchamber.org
info@keywestchamber.org

Marine Protected Area Contacts

The Florida Keys are encompassed by a network of marine protected areas that have been established over the years by both state and federal agencies (see map, page 128). The areas are listed under a variety of names—including parks, sanctuaries, refuges and reserves—but all have one purpose: to safeguard the natural, cultural and historic resources of the Keys. Regulations pertaining to diving and snorkeling are summarized on page 127. For more detailed information or to find out how you can help, please contact the appropriate office listed below:

Biscayne National Park
9700 SW 328th St.
Homestead, FL 33033-5634
☎ 230-7275 fax: 230-1190
www.nps.gov/bisc
BISC_Information@nps.gov

Everglades National Park
40001 State Road 9336
Homestead, FL 33034-6733
☎ 242-7700 fax: 242-7728
www.nps.gov/ever
EVER_Information@nps.gov

**Florida Keys National
   Marine Sanctuary**
P.O. Box 500368
Marathon, FL 33050
☎ 743-2437 fax: 743-2357
www.fknms.nos.noaa.gov
floridakeys@nms.noaa.gov

FKNMS Upper Keys Region
P.O. Box 1083
Key Largo, FL 33037
☎ 852-7717 fax: 853-0877

FKNMS Lower Keys Region
216 Ann St.
Key West, FL 33040
☎ 292-0311 fax: 292-5065

**John Pennekamp Coral Reef
   State Park**
P.O. Box 487
Key Largo, FL 33037
☎ 451-1202
www.dep.state.fl.us/parks/district_
   5/JohnPennekamp/index.htm

National Key Deer Refuge
(includes Crocodile Lake National
Wildlife Refuge, Great White Heron
National Wildlife Refuge and Key
West National Wildlife Refuge)
P.O. Box 430510
Big Pine Key, FL 33043-0510
☎ 872-2239
http://refuges.southeast.fws.gov/
   nationalkeydeer/index.html

Dry Tortugas National Park
P.O. Box 6208
Key West, FL 33041
☎ 242-7700 fax: 242-7711
www.nps.gov/drto
DRTO_Information@nps.gov

Index

dive sites covered in this book appear in **bold** type

A

accommodations 25
activities and attractions 27-31
Adolphus Busch Sr. 102-103
air travel 19
Alicia 43
Alligator, USS 84
Alligator Reef 84
Aquarius underwater laboratory 78-79
Avanti see **Windjammer**

B

Bahia Honda State Park 95
Banana Reef 61
Barge, The *see* **Flagler's Barge**
barracuda 125
beaches 9, 47, 76, 85, 95, 114
Benwood 64-65
Benwood's **Outside Wall** 65
Bibb 72-73
bicycling 21
Biscayne National Park 42
Black Caesar 42-43
bristle worm 123
business hours 24

C

Cannonball Cut 103
canoeing 27-28
Carysford, HMS *see* **Carysfort Reef**
Carysfort Reef 51-52
cave dives 65
Cayman Salvage Master 108-109
certification 37-38
chambers of commerce 139
Christ of the Abyss 60
Christ of the Deep 59-60
Christmas Tree Cave 66
City of Washington 54
Civil War Wreck 53
climate 18
Coffins Patch 87
Conch Reef 78
Conch Republic 110
Conchs 14, 110
Conch Wall 77
coral spawning 102
Cressi, Egidi 60
Crocker Reef 82
currency *see* money
Curry Hammock State Park 85

D

Davis Reef 81
Delta Shoal 93-94
Delta Shoal Barge *see* **Flagler's Barge**
dining 25-26
dive boat evaluation 33
dive gear 23, 133
dive operator evaluation 132
Divers Alert Network 34-35
dive site icons 39
dive training 37-38
diving and flying 32
diving conditions 36-37
diving services 132-137
dolphin encounters 28-29
Dry Tortugas 114-119, 126
Duane 73-74

E

Eagle 82-83
Eastern Dry Rocks 109
ecology 12-14
Elbow, The 55
electricity 22
expertise levels 40

F

fire coral 123
Fire Coral Caves 71
fish feeding 91
fishing 29
Flagler, Henry 15
Flagler's Barge 92-93
Florida Keys National Marine
   Sanctuary 127-129
food 25-26
Fort Jefferson 114, 118, 126
Fort Jefferson Moat Wall 118
French Reef 65-66
French Wreck *see* **Windjammer**

G

Galletti, Guido 60
Gap, The 89
geography 11
geology 11-12
glass-bottom boats 27
gloves 23
Grecian Rocks (Back Reef) 61-62
Grecian Rocks (Fore Reef) 60-61

H

Hard Bottom Cave 66
Hardee, Ellison 60
Haystacks 103-104
hazardous marine life 123-125
health 32-35
Hen & Chickens 80-81
Herman's Hole 91-92
history 14-15
Hole in the Wall 71
Horseshoe Reef 56
hotels *see* accommodations
Hourglass Cave 66
hurricanes 15, 18, 30, 83, 105, 109
hyperbaric chambers 35

I

insects 32
Islamorada 46
Ivory Coast Wreck *see* **Delta Shoal**

J

jellyfish 123
Joe's Tug 105
John Pennekamp 126
John Pennekamp Coral Reef State Park 47,
   59-60, 126-127
Jules' Undersea Lodge 25

K

kayaking 27-28
Key deer 96
Key Largo 46-47
Key Largo Dry Rocks 59-60
Key Largo National Marine Sanctuary 127
Key West 14-15, 30-31, 95-97
Key West Aquarium 30
Key West National Wildlife Refuge
   see **Marquesas Keys**
Keys Association of Dive Operators 133

L

language 18-19
lighthouses 15, 31, 51, 84, 94, 111
Little Grecian 61-62
Little Palm Island *see* **Newfound Harbor**
live-aboards 39, 138
Long Reef 43
Looe, HMS *see* **Looe Key (East End)**
Looe Key (Deep) 100
Looe Key (East End) 98-99
Looe Key National Marine
   Sanctuary 98-101, 127
Looe Key (West End) 99-100

Lounge, The 103-104
Lower Keys 95-113
Lower Keys Underwater Music Festival 100
Lugana 43

M

Maine, USS *see City of Washington*
Mallory Square 31, 97
Mandalay 43
mangrove forests 14
maps
   dive site maps
      Biscayne National Park 42
      Dry Tortugas 115
      Key Largo 49
      Lower Keys 96-97
      Middle Keys 86
      Plantation & Upper Matecumbe Keys 76
   Florida Keys National Marine Sanctuary 128
   Greater Miami 20
   highlights map 16-17
   locator map 9
   map index 41
Marathon 85-86
marine conservation organizations 131
marine life 120-122
marine protected area contacts 140
marine reserves 126-129, 140
maritime museums 30-31
Marker 1 *see* **Toppino's Buoy**
Marker 32 *see* **Toppino's Buoy**
Marquesas Keys 113
measurement 22-23
medical facilities 35
Miami 19-21
Middle Keys 85-94
mile markers 21
Molasses Reef (Deep) 70
Molasses Reef (North End) 68
Molasses Reef (South End) 71
money 22
moorings 130
moray eel 124

N

National Key Deer Refuge 96
Newfound Harbor 98
9-Foot Stake 107-108
North Dry Rocks 58
North North Dry Rocks 57
Nuestra Señora de Atocha 30-31, 113

O

Overseas Highway 11, 15
Overseas Railroad 15

P

parasailing 28
Perky's Bat Tower 96
Permit Ledge 71
photography, underwater 23-24
Pickle Barrel Wreck *see* **Pickles**
Pickles 74
Pigeon Key 95
pirates 42-43
Plantation Key 75-76
Ponce de León 14
population 11
pre-trip preparation 32-34
public boat ramps 138

Q

queen conch 14, 78

R

recompression chambers 35
Reef Environmental Education Foundation 61
reef terminology 37
resorts *see* accommodations
responsible diving 129-131
restaurants *see* dining
Rock Key 110

S

sailing 30
Samatha's Reef 90
sanctuary regulations 127
Sand Bottom Cave 66
Sand Island 67-68
Sand Key Reef 111
scorpionfish 124
sea urchin 124
Seven Mile Bridge 95
shark 125
Sherwood Forest 116-117
shopping 26
shore dives 118
signaling devices 34
snorkeling 38
snorkeling sites 43, 44, 50-52, 54-61, 64-68,
    71, 74, 78, 80, 81, 84, 87, 90-94, 98, 99, 103,
    106, 107, 109-113, 118, 119
Sombrero Reef 94
South Carysfort Reef 52

Spanish Anchor 71
Spiegel Grove 62-63
state parks 30, 138-139
Statue, The *see* **Key Largo Dry Rocks**
stingray 125
Stock Island 96
sunset celebration 31

T

telephone calls 132
Texas Rock 117-118
Three Sisters 66-67
Thunderbolt 88
time 22
Tonawanda see **The Elbow**
Toppino's Buoy 106-107
transportation 21-22
Turtle Rocks 50-51
Turtle Reef *see* **Turtle Rocks**
turtles 50

U

Upper Keys 46-84
Upper Matecumbe Key 46, 75-76

V

Virginia Reef 44

W

Wall, The 45
water color 12
Wellwood, MV *see* **Molasses Reef (North End)**
Western Dry Rocks 112-113
Western Sambo 103-104
what to bring 23
White Bank Coral Garden *see* **White Bank
    (North & South)**
White Bank Dry Rocks *see* **White Bank
    (North & South)**
White Bank (North & South) 66
Winch Hole 71
Windjammer 119
wreck dives 43, 53-56, 62, 64, 71-74, 82-84, 88,
    92-94, 98, 102, 105, 108, 119
wreck diving 63
wrecking 15

Lonely Planet Pisces Books

The **Diving & Snorkeling** guides cover top destinations worldwide. Beautifully illustrated with full-color photos throughout, the series explores the best diving and snorkeling areas and prepares divers for what to expect when they get there. Each site is described in detail, with information on suggested ability levels, depth, visibility and, of course, marine life. There's basic topside information as well for each destination.

Also check out dive guides to:

Australia's Great Barrier Reef

Australia: Southeast Coast

Bali & Lombok

Baja California

Bermuda

Bonaire

Chuuk Lagoon, Pohnpei & Kosrae

Cocos Island

Curaçao

Guam & Yap

Jamaica

Monterey Peninsula & Northern California

Pacific Northwest

Palau

Papua New Guinea

Red Sea

Roatan & Honduras' Bay Islands

Scotland

Seychelles

Tahiti & French Polynesia

Texas

Thailand

Turks & Caicos

Vanuatu